Series Editor:
Paul Wehman, Ph.D.

The Brookes
Transition to
Adulthood Series

EVIDENCE-BASED
Instructional
Strategies FOR
Transition

Also in *The Brookes
Transition to Adulthood Series:*

Essentials of Transition Planning

Paul Wehman, Ph.D.
with invited contributors

*Transition Planning for Culturally and
Linguistically Diverse Youth*

Gary Greene, Ph.D.

The Brookes
Transition to
Adulthood Series

EVIDENCE-BASED
Instructional
Strategies FOR
Transition

by

David W. Test, Ph.D.
The University of North Carolina at Charlotte

with invited contributors

·P·A·U·L·H·
BROOKES
PUBLISHING C<u>O</u>®

Baltimore • London • Sydney

Paul H. Brookes Publishing Co.
Post Office Box 10624
Baltimore, Maryland 21285-0624
USA

www.brookespublishing.com

Typeset by Auburn Associates, Inc., Baltimore, Maryland.
Manufactured in the United States of America by
Sheridan Books, Inc., Chelsea, Michigan.

The individuals described in this book are composites or real people whose situations are masked and are based on the authors' experiences. In all instances, names and identifying details have been changed to protect confidentiality.

Library of Congress Cataloging-in-Publication Data

Test, David Wesley, 1953–
   Evidence-based instructional strategies for transition / by David W. Test; with invited contributors.
        p.   cm. – (The Brookes transition to adulthood series)
   Includes bibliographical references and index.
   ISBN-13: 978-1-59857-192-9
   ISBN-10: 1-59857-192-3
   1. Teenagers with disabilities–Education–United States.   2. Teenagers with disabilities Vocational guidance–United States.   I. Title.
   LC4031.T43   2012
   371.9–dc23   2011026876

British Library Cataloguing in Publication data are available from the British Library.

2015   2014   2013   2012   2011

10   9   8   7   6   5   4   3   2   1

Contents

Series Preface

The Brookes Transition to Adulthood Series was developed for the purpose of meeting the critical educational needs of students with disabilities who will be moving from school to adulthood. It is no longer acceptable to simply equip a student with a set of isolated life skills that may or may not be relevant to his or her adult life. Nor is it sufficient to treat the student as if he or she will remain unchanged throughout life. As we allow for growth and change in real-life environments, so must we allow for growth and change in the individuals who will operate within the environments. Today, transition must concern itself with the whole life pattern of each student as it relates to his or her future. However, integrating the two constructs of self and the real adult world for one student at a time is not always straightforward. It requires skills and knowledge. It requires a well-thought-out, well-orchestrated team effort. It takes individualization, ingenuity, perseverance, and more.

The results of these first-rate efforts can be seen when they culminate in a student with a disability who exits school prepared to move to his or her life beyond the classroom. Unfortunately, though, this does not always happen. This is because transition has become a splintered concept, too weighted down by process and removed from building on the student's aspirations and desires for "a good life." However, it does not have to be this way.

This book series is designed to help the teachers, transition specialists, rehabilitation counselors, community service providers, administrators, policy makers, other professionals, and families who are looking for useful information on a daily basis by translating the evidence-based transition research into practice. Each volume addresses specific objectives that are related to the all-important and overarching goal of helping students meet the demands of school and society and gain a greater understanding of themselves so that they are equipped for success in the adult world.

Editorial
Advisory Board

About the Author

David W. Test, Ph.D., Professor of Special Education at the University of North Carolina (UNC) at Charlotte, teaches courses in single-subject research, transition, classroom management, and professional writing. The majority of Dr. Test's publications have focused on self-determination, transition, community-based training, and supported employment. Along with Dr. Nellie Aspel and Dr. Jane Everson, he wrote the first transition methods textbook, titled *Transition Methods for Youth with Disabilities* (Merrill/Prentice Hall, 2006). Dr. Test currently serves as a co-principal investigator (with Dr. Paula Kohler and Dr. Larry Kortering) of the National Secondary Transition Technical Assistance Center, Co-Director on the North Carolina Indicator 14, Post-school Outcomes Project and the CIRCLES interagency collaboration Institute of Education Sciences research grant (with Dr. Claudia Flowers), and the UNC Charlotte Doctoral Leadership Personnel Preparation Program (with Dr. Diane Browder). He and Dr. Bob Algozzine currently serve as co-editors of *Career Development for Exceptional Individuals.*

About the Contributors

Audrey Bartholomew, M.Ed., is currently pursuing her doctorate from the University of North Carolina at Charlotte, where she is a graduate research assistant for the National Secondary Transition Technical Assistance Center. She has taught students with moderate to severe disabilities in middle and high school. Her research interests include self-determination, employment, and alignment of transition and standards-based education for students with disabilities.

Melissa Hudson, M.A.Ed., is a graduate research associate and doctoral student in special education at the University of North Carolina (UNC) at Charlotte. Her research interests include general curriculum access, alternate assessment based on alternate achievement standards, and evidence-based practices for students with significant intellectual disability. Before beginning the doctoral program at UNC Charlotte, Melissa taught students with severe intellectual disability in Kentucky for 10 years.

Kelly Kelley, M.A.Ed., is completing her dissertation in a postsecondary educational setting using technology to teach pedestrian navigation skills to young adults with intellectual disabilities. She has published or copublished three book chapters, six refereed journal publications, and three online publications and has presented at more than 15 national or international conferences. Her research interests include secondary transition relating to employment, independent living, and inclusive postsecondary opportunities for individuals with moderate developmental/intellectual disabilities.

Larry Kortering, Ed.D., is Professor of Special Education at Appalachian State University in Boone, North Carolina. His research and related work focuses on school completion and best practices in transition services for youth with disabilities, with an emphasis on developing interventions and services that prove responsive to the student consumer.

Valerie L. Mazzotti, Ph.D., is Assistant Professor of Special Education at Western Carolina University in Cullowhee, North Carolina. Dr. Mazzotti received her doctorate in special education from the University of North Carolina at Charlotte. As a classroom teacher, Dr. Mazzotti taught students with disabilities in resource and inclusion settings. Her current research interests include students with high-incidence disabilities, self-determination, positive behavior supports, and evidence-based practices.

April L. Mustian, Ph.D., is Assistant Professor of Special Education at Illinois State University. She received her doctorate in Special Education at the University of North Carolina at Charlotte. During her doctoral studies, she worked as a project staff member with the National Transition Technical Assistance Center, a technical assistance and dissemination center funded by the Office of Special Education Programs, to help states build capacity to support and improve transition planning, services, and outcomes for youth with disabilities. Her research experience and interests include academic and behavioral interventions for students with and at risk for emotional disturbance, applied behavior analysis, positive behavior support, and secondary transition.

Sharon M. Richter, Ph.D., is Assistant Professor of Special Education at Appalachian State University in Boone, North Carolina. She teaches a variety of courses, including content related to secondary transition and students with intellectual disabilities. Her current research interests include identifying strategies to facilitate postsecondary success among youth with intellectual disabilities.

Dawn A. Rowe, M.A., is a doctoral student working on her Ph.D. in Special Education at the University of North Carolina at Charlotte. Her current interests include parent and family involvement in special education, interagency collaboration, and transition from school to adult life for students with disabilities.

Nicole Uphold, Ph.D., was a high school teacher for students with moderate to severe intellectual disabilities. Prior to that, she worked as vocational rehabilitation counselor, assisting students with disabilities with transitioning from school to employment. She is currently Assistant Professor of Special Education at Illinois State University, where her research interests include the transition from school to adult life, teaching self-determination skills to students with disabilities, and personnel preparation.

Allison Walker, Ph.D., earned her doctorate from the University of North Carolina at Charlotte. She is Assistant Professor of Special Education at the University of North Carolina at Wilmington and teaches courses in transition, consultation and collaboration, and secondary methods. Her research interests include identifying evidence-based practices in secondary transition, multiculturalism and transition, and self-determination.

Acknowledgments

I am honored to have been asked to write this text as part of *The Brookes Transition to Adulthood Series*. The work is the product of a lifelong commitment to improving the lives of young adults with disabilities, culminating with being funded as the National Secondary Transition Technical Assistance Center (NSTTAC; Grant H326J050004). As the U.S. Department of Education, Office of Special Education Program's federally funded technical assistance and dissemination center for secondary transition, one of NSTTAC's purposes has been to identify, compile, and disseminate the evidence base on what works in secondary transition to help schools improve their capacity to provide quality secondary transition services. As a result, I would like to thank my other NSTTAC codirectors, Paula Kohler and Larry Kortering, and our Project Officer, Marlene Simon-Burroughs. I would also like to thank Catherine Fowler, without whom NSTTAC and I could not function.

I would also like to acknowledge my contributors and coauthors, Audrey Bartholomew, Melissa Hudson, Kelly Kelley, Larry Kortering (again), Valerie Mazzotti, April Mustian, Sharon Richter, Dawn Rowe, Nicole Uphold, and Allison Walker. Without them, this task would have been too much. I appreciate their willingness to do good work with limited input from me.

Next, I would like to thank *The Brookes Transition to Adulthood Series* Editorial Advisory Board for their support and excellent comments and suggestions. The text is much improved thanks to you. In additional, a special thank you goes to Paul Wehman for inviting me to be part of this endeavor and to Rebecca Lazo, Senior Acquisitions Editor at Paul H. Brookes Publishing Co., for talking me into doing the text; Steve Plocher, Associate Editor, for keeping me on task while Rebecca started a family; and Cathy Jewell, Project Manager, for her timely feedback.

Finally, I would like to thank all my past and current students and colleagues for teaching me that secondary transition is truly a collaborative effort. I learned more from you than you can imagine. Thanks.

To our families

1

Transition-Focused Education

David W. Test

The school years can be viewed as a series of transitions: from preschool to elementary school, elementary to middle school, middle school to high school, and high school to employment or postsecondary education. All of these transitions come with anxiety and rewards, probably none so much as the transition from high school to postsecondary education and employment, which some might call *adulthood*. Halpern provided an excellent definition of this time period as "a period of floundering that occurs for at least the first several years after leaving school as adolescents attempt to assume a variety of adult roles in their communities" (1992, p. 203). With this in mind, it makes sense that the purpose of secondary transition is to design services and supports to help students with disabilities make as smooth a transition as possible–what some authors have called a seamless transition (Rusch & Braddock, 2004). The goal is for the day after graduation to be no different than the day before (Certo et al., 2008).

As a way to help students avoid floundering and achieve a seamless transition from high school to adulthood, Kohler and Field (2003) introduced the concept of *transition-focused education*. Transition-focused education has the goal of preparing students for success in their post-school lives. It is guided by each student's desired post-school goals and consists of "academic, career, and transition approaches and services, depending on the local interest and student's learning and support needs" (Kohler & Field, 2003, p. 176). A brief review of the history of legislation related to secondary transition will help readers understand the importance of the concept of transition-focused education.

Halpern described secondary transition as "old wine in new bottles" (1992, p. 202) with its roots in the cooperative work study programs of the 1960s and the career education movement of the 1970s. Secondary transition was formally recognized in 1984 by Madeleine Will, who was then the director of the Office of Special Education and Rehabilitation Services, as an important part of the lives of all individuals with disabilities. In her seminal writing, Will described secondary transition as a set of three possible bridges students could use to move from high school to employment.

> [Transition is an] outcome-oriented process encompassing a broad array of services and experiences that lead to employment. Transition is a period that includes high school, the point of graduation, additional postsecondary education or adult ser-

vices, and the initial years of employment. Transition is a bridge between the security and structure offered by the school and the opportunities and risks of adult life. Any bridge requires both a solid span and a secure foundation at either end. The transition for school to work and adult life requires sound preparation in the secondary school, adequate support at the point of school leaving, and secure opportunities and services, if needed, in adult situations. (1984, p. 2)

Will's definition quickly became known as the *bridges model* (see Figure 1.1), which includes three different paths or bridges:

1. No *special services*, which refers to services available to anyone in the community (e.g., community college)

2. *Time-limited services*, which refers to services specifically designated for individuals with disabilities (e.g., vocational rehabilitation)

3. *Ongoing services*, which refers to services available to an individual throughout his or her life (e.g., supported employment)

Although the bridges model provides an excellent starting point, there is more to life than just work. As a result, Halpern (1985) introduced an alternative model that expanded the transition from high school to community adjustment (see Figure 1.2). Halpern's model of community adjustment not only included employment, but it also included residential environments and social and interpersonal networks.

Although Will (1984) and Halpern (1985) drew attention to the need for formal secondary transition services, it was not until the passage of the Individuals with Disabilities Education Act (IDEA) of 1990 (PL 101-476) that transition services for all students with dis-

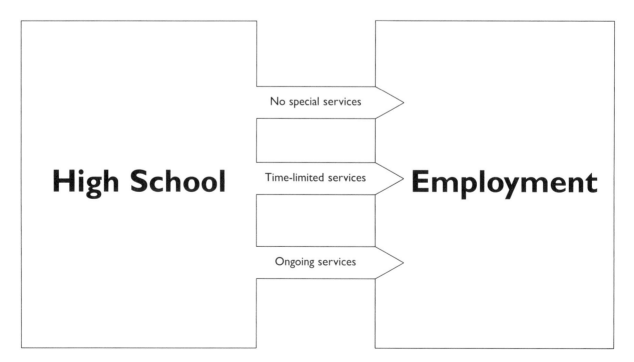

Figure 1.1. The bridges model. (From Will, M. [1984]. Bridges from school to working life. *Programs for the Handicapped.* Washington, DC: Clearinghouse on the Handicapped.)

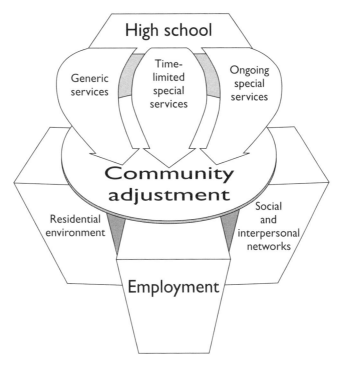

Figure 1.2. The transition model. (From Halpern, A. [1985]. Transition: A look at the foundations. *Exceptional Children, 51,* 481; reprinted by permission.)

abilities were mandated. For the first time, transition services were defined, student individualized education programs (IEPs) were required to have a transition component beginning not later than age 16, and youth with disabilities were to be provided with coordinated services that linked students with adult service providers as needed.

The IDEA Amendments of 1997 (PL 105-17) further improved the delivery of transition services through a series of changes. First, transition services were expanded to include related services. Second, the IEP had to include a statement of transition services beginning at age 14. Finally, a year prior to each student reaching the age of majority in their state, their IEP was to include a statement that the student was informed that rights would be transferred.

IDEA 2004 (PL 108-446) reauthorized and again strengthened requirements for transition services. First, transition services were defined as the following:

> A coordinated set of activities for a child with a disability that is designed to be within a results-oriented process, that is focused on improving the academic and functional achievement of the child with a disability to facilitate the child's movement from school to post-school activities including post-secondary education, vocational education, integrated employment (including supported employment), continuing and adult education, adult services, independent living, or community participation; is based on the individuals child's needs, taking into account the child's strengths, preferences, and interests; and includes instruction, related services, community experiences, the development of employment and other post-school adult living objectives, and when appropriate, acquisition of daily living skills and functional vocational evaluation. (20 U.S.C. § 1401[602][34])

Specifically, according to IDEA 2004, vocational education should be considered a transition service; the goal of secondary education should be to prepare students for successful post-school education, employment, and independent living; and schools should provide each student with a summary of performance at the point of graduation from high school. Unfortunately, IDEA 2004 changed the required age for starting transition services back to no later than age 16. However, because each state had the right to require an earlier starting point, many states kept the age at 14. Because of this, the reader should find out what is required in his or her own state.

Also new with IDEA 2004 was a set of accountability procedures for states to follow. This accountability process involved each state writing a state performance plan (SPP) and then providing an annual performance report (APR) to the U.S. Department of Education's Office of Special Education Programs. The resulting 20 SPP/APR performance indicators related to Part B of IDEA (children with disabilities ages 3–22) included reporting four sets of data specifically related to secondary transition for students with disabilities, including graduation rates (Indicator 1), dropout rates (Indicator 2), IEP transition services (Indicator 13), and post-school outcomes for students moving from secondary to postsecondary settings (Indicator 14). Because Indicator 13 is the IEP transition indicator, it is important to understand its relevance for state and local education agencies. Indicator 13 states that each student's IEP must include

> Appropriate measureable postsecondary goals that are annually updated and based upon an age-appropriate transition assessment, transition services, including courses of study, that will reasonably enable the student to meet those postsecondary goals, and annual IEP goals related to the student's transition services needs. There also must be evidence that the student was invited to the IEP Team meeting where transition services are to be discussed and evidence that, if appropriate, a representative of any participation agency was invited to the IEP Team meeting with the prior consent of the parent or student who has reached the age of majority. (20 U.S.C. § 1416[a][3][B])

To help states and local agencies evaluate student IEPs to ensure compliance with Indicator 13, the National Secondary Transition Technical Assistance Center (NSTTAC) developed an eight-item checklist. This checklist is described in more detail in Chapter 2.

TAXONOMY FOR TRANSITION PROGRAMMING

Given the enormous responsibility of providing students with disabilities with an individualized set of transition services from the vast array of possible supports and services, it is useful to have a framework for organizing effective practices. One such framework is the Taxonomy for Transition Programming, which was developed by Kohler (1996) to provide the field of secondary transition with an applied framework for organizing secondary practices associated with improving post-school outcomes for youth with disabilities (see Figure 1.3). This Taxonomy for Transition Programming was an outgrowth of a series of related studies, including a metaevaluation of the program activities and outcomes of federally funded model demonstration transition programs (Rusch, Kohler, & Hughes, 1992), a review of the literature (Kohler, 1993), an analysis of exemplary transition programs (Kohler, DeStefano, Wermuth, Grayson, & McGinty, 1994), and concept mapping (Kohler, 1996). The resulting Taxonomy for Transition Programming includes five major categories and

Figure 1.3. The Taxonomy for Transition Programming. (From Kohler, P.D. [1996]. *Taxonomy for transition programming* [p. 3]. Champaign: University of Illinois. *Key:* IEP, individualized education program.)

serves as the foundation for the remaining chapters in this text. Each category is described in the following sections. Table 1.1 includes a set of reflective questions that can be used to help readers think about improving transition services for students with disabilities in their schools.

Student-Focused Planning

Student-focused planning practices include using assessment information and facilitating students' self-determination to develop individual education programs based on students' post-school goals. The major components include IEP development, student participation, and planning strategies. See Chapters 2 and 5 for instructional strategies related to this category.

Table 1.1. Sample reflective questions for taxonomy categories

Student-focused planning

To what extent do students and parents actively participate in individualized education program (IEP) development? Do students have knowledge and skills to participate actively? How are students' interests, needs, and preferences determined and documented?

To what extent and how are academic, cognitive, and/or adaptive behavior assessment information used in developing educational goals and objectives and determining related service needs? To what extent and how is information gathered through career awareness and exploration activities linked to a student's IEPs and/or career plans?

To what extent are goals and objectives identified in IEPs (including transition services) implemented and evaluated?

What strategies are used to ensure students, parents, and agency personnel actively participate in IEP meetings? How is participation measured? What are the findings?

To what extent and how are the responsibilities assigned through the IEP process reviewed? To what extent do identified services go undelivered? What procedures are used to address discrepancies between services promised and services provided?

Student development

To what extent do students enroll in and complete occupational-specific programs? What specific services do students receive that support their access and participation in occupational programs? What services do they need but do not receive?

What assessment information is collected and used in students' IEP development? How is this information compiled and used in planning students' educational program and services? Are student portfolios used to collect and organize information? What information do they include?

To what extent do students with disabilities participate in paid work experiences during high school? In which occupational areas are they employed?

What curricula or strategies are used to teach students skills related to social interactions, self-determination, and independent living? How effective are these curricula? How are students' skills measured?

Are students recruited and to what extent do they participate in vocational student organizations and other cocurricular and extracurricular activities?

Interagency collaboration

How and to what extent do various disciplines (e.g., vocational education, special education) and service agencies (e.g., educational, rehabilitation) coordinate, collect, and share assessment information?

To what extent do local communities have a local coordinating council that addresses community-level service issues?

How many schools have up-to-date collaborative agreements with their local rehabilitation agency? To what extent do rehabilitation counselors meet with students in schools? To what extent do rehabilitation counselors actively participate in IEP meetings? How many students are receiving rehabilitation services? What services are they receiving? What services do they need but not receive? How many and what services are projected for the future?

Family involvement

To what extent and how are parents and/or families of students with disabilities included in professional development activities and program planning, implementation, and evaluation? In what roles do family members participate in providing transition-related education and services? What strategies are used to recruit and/or involve family members?

How satisfied are parents and family members with their involvement in professional development activities and program planning, implementation, and evaluation? How do parents and families perceive the effectiveness of transition-focused education and services for their children?

To what extent are training opportunities provided for parents and family members? How effective are these activities in increasing parents' knowledge and skills? Do these activities positively influence the extent to which parents and/or family members are involved in transition-related education and service delivery?

Program structures and attributes

Are students' post-school outcomes measured? What outcomes do students achieve with respect to employment, independent living, social and recreation, and community participation?

What incentives and/or disincentives are used to hold schools accountable for students' post-school outcomes? To what extent and how are student outcomes considered in the monitoring and/or quality assurance processes?

To what extent and how are specific transition-related teacher competencies included in the licensure and certification standards (e.g., ability to teach self-determination, strategies for facilitating active student involvement in IEP planning, understanding of rehabilitation and adult services systems, ability to work collaboratively with rehabilitation counselors and adult agency personnel)? Are these competencies addressed in teacher and/or administrator assessments and mentor programs? Do practicing and beginning teachers (academic, special, and vocational) possess these competencies?

To what extent is a transition-focused education philosophy reflected in state and local vision statements? What are local schools' expectations for their students with disabilities?

How are transition services perceived at the local level (i.e., narrowly defined or broadly interpreted)? What barriers impede the adoption of a broad transition perspective? How are state transition and school-to-work initiatives perceived and implemented at the local level (e.g., separate, competing, parallel, integrated)?

Are local resources adequate to meet the education and transition service needs of all their students?

From Kohler, P.D. (1996). *Taxonomy for transition programming.* Champaign: University of Illinois.

Student Development

Student development practices emphasize life, employment, and occupational skill development through school-based and work-based learning experiences. Student assessment and accommodations provide a fundamental basis for student development that results in successful transition. This is an important category because it includes both student assessment and student instruction in transition skills and (although not explicitly stated) academic skills. See Chapters 2, 4, and 6–8 for instructional practices related to this category.

Interagency Collaboration

Interagency collaboration practices facilitate involvement of community businesses, organizations, and agencies in all aspects of transition-focused education. Strategies in this category include developing interagency agreements that clearly articulate roles, responsibilities, communication strategies, and other collaborative actions that enhance curricula and program development to foster collaboration.

Family Involvement

Family involvement practices are associated with parent and family involvement in planning and delivering education and transition services. Family-focused training and family empowerment activities increase the ability of family members to work effectively with educators and other service providers.

Program Structures

Program structures are features that relate to efficient and effective delivery of transition-focused education and services, including philosophy, planning, policy, evaluation, and human resource development. The structures of a school provide the framework for transition-focused education practices to occur.

Although this book does not focus directly on the taxonomy categories of interagency collaboration, family involvement, and program structures, the assessment and instructional practices described in the remaining chapters could not be implemented without these categories occurring.

TRANSITION-FOCUSED EDUCATION
AND STANDARDS-BASED EDUCATION

Although transition services are mandated by law and are seemingly critically important for helping students with disabilities achieve their desired post-school outcomes, standards-based educational movements such as high-stakes testing, increased graduation requirements, and common standards are often seen as barriers to providing quality transition services. However, transition-focused education can bridge the apparent gap between an academic and transition-related school focus. Kochhar-Bryant and Bassett suggested that transition-focused education could be used as a decision-making framework that considers current curricula and supports needed for all students to achieve their stated post-school goals.

> Transition is not just a program or a project or a set of activities that has a beginning and end. It is a vision and goal for unfolding the fullest possible potential for an individual and a systematic framework for planning to fulfill that potential. (2002, p. 19)

This goal can be met for all students if schools use transition-focused education.

Since first being reported in the 1980s (e.g., Hasazi, Gordon, & Roe, 1985), post-school outcomes for students with disabilities have been consistently poor compared with individuals without disabilities in the areas of education, employment, and independent living (Blackorby & Wagner, 1996; Wagner, Newman, Cameto, Garza, & Levine, 2005). For example, 45% of youth with disabilities reportedly pursued postsecondary education within 4 years of leaving high school compared with 53% of youth without disabilities. In terms of employment, 57% of youth with disabilities leaving high school were employed outside the home compared with 67% of youth without disabilities. In addition, 25% of youth with disabilities were reported to be living independently compared with 28% of youth without disabilities (Newman, Wagner, Cameto, & Knokey, 2009). Post-school outcomes for students with disabilities still have room for improvement. One solution to this problem could be the use of evidence-based instructional practices.

Evidence-based practices are an outgrowth of educational legislation requiring teachers to use scientifically based instructional strategies. First, the No Child Left Behind (NCLB) Act of 2001 (PL 107-110) stated schools must ensure that all students have access to effective instructional strategies derived from scientifically based research. Scientifically based research was defined as research that involved the use of "rigorous, systematic, and objective procedures to obtain reliable and valid knowledge relevant to education activities and programs" (20 U.S.C. § 7901[37]). Next, IDEA 2004 reinforced this by calling for the use of scientifically based instruction with students with disabilities. In response to the legislation, in a special issue of *Exceptional Children*, Odom et al. (2005) used the term *evidence-based practices* to refer to educational practices that had been demonstrated effective based on quality research. In the same issue, Horner et al. defined a practice as "a curriculum, behavioral intervention, systems, changes, or educational approach

Research by Hasazi, Gordon, and Roe (1985) was one of a series of post-school outcomes studies published in the 1980s. The study reported that although 50%–60% of students with disabilities were employed, only 20%–30% were employed full time. In addition, about 50% of students with disabilities earned a salary at or below minimum wage, and most did not receive fringe benefits.

designed for use by…with the express expectation that implementation will result in measureable educational, social, behavioral, or physical benefit" (2005, p. 175).

What this meant for schools and teachers is that in order to meet the NCLB and IDEA requirements, instructional practices must be based on high-quality experimental research. Also in the special issue of *Exceptional Children,* Gersten et al. (2005) suggested quality indicators for group and quasi-experimental research design, and Horner et al. (2005) suggested quality indicators for single-subject experimental research designs.

The NSTTAC conducted a comprehensive literature review to identify evidence-based secondary transition practices (Test et al., 2009a). Using criteria for high-quality research and evidence-based practice suggested by Gersten et al. (2005) and Horner et al. (2005), the review identified 64 secondary transition practices. See Table 1.2 for a list of secondary transition evidence-based practices categorized by the Taxonomy for Transition Programming.

Table 1.2. Evidence-based practices organized by the taxonomy for transition programming

Student-focused planning

Using *check and connect* to promote student participation in the individualized education program (IEP) meeting

Using *computer-assisted instruction* to teach student participation in the IEP meeting

Using *published curricula* to teach student involvement in the IEP

Using the *self-advocacy strategy* to teach student participation in the IEP meeting

Using the *self-directed IEP* to teach student participation in the IEP meeting

Using *whose future is it anyway?* to teach student knowledge of transition planning

Student development

Using *backward chaining* to teach functional life skills

Using *computer-assisted instruction* to teach food preparation and cooking skills, grocery shopping skills, and job-specific skills

Using *technology* to teach academic skills

Using *community-based instruction* to teach banking skills, grocery shopping skills, community integration skills, purchasing skills, safety skills, communication skills, and employment skills

Using *constant time delay* to teach banking skills, food preparation and cooking skills, functional life skills, leisure skills, and job-specific skills

Using an *extension of career planning services after graduation* to promote increased finance skills

Using *forward chaining* to teach home maintenance skills

Using the *one more than strategy* to teach counting money and purchasing skills

Using *peer-assisted instruction* to teach academic skills

Using *progressive time delay* to teach purchasing skills, safety skills, and functional life skills

Using *response prompting* to teach food preparation and cooking skills, grocery shopping skills, home maintenance skills, laundry tasks, leisure skills, purchasing skills, sight word reading, social skills, and employment skills

Using *mnemonics* to teach completing a job application and academic skills

Using *static picture prompts* to teach purchasing skills

Using *video modeling* to teach food preparation, cooking, and home maintenance skills

Using *visual displays* to teach academic skills

Using the *self-determined learning model of instruction* to teach goal attainment

Using *self-management instruction* to teach academic skills, social skills, and job-specific skills

Using *self-monitoring instruction* to teach functional life skills

Using *simulations* to teach banking skills, purchasing skills, and social skills

Using a *system of least-to-most prompts* to teach food preparation and cooking skills, grocery shopping skills, purchasing skills, safety skills, functional life skills, communication skills, and specific job skills

Using a *system of most-to-least prompts* to teach functional life skills

(continued)

Table 1.2. *(continued)*

Using *total task chaining* to teach functional life skills

Using *whose future is it anyway?* to teach self-determination skills

Family involvement

Using *training modules* to promote parent involvement in the transition process

Program structures

Using *check and connect* to promote student participation in the IEP meeting

Using *community-based instruction* to teach banking skills, grocery shopping skills, community integration skills, purchasing skills, safety skills, communication skills, and employment skills

Using an *extension of career planning services after graduation* to promote increased finance skills

Although these evidence-based practices are designed to teach students specific transition-related skills, the experimental studies on which they were based did not measure the impact of these skills on post-school outcomes. As a result, Test, Mazzotti, et al. (2009c) conducted a second literature review that included rigorous correlational research in secondary transition to identify the evidence-based predictors that correlated with improved post-school outcomes in education, employment, or independent living. Based on results of this review, 16 evidence-based, in-school predictors of post-school outcomes were identified (see Table 1.3). Together, these evidence-based instructional practices and predictors provide educators with the building blocks needed to construct a quality, transition-focused education program. They also serve as the foundation for all practices described throughout this book.

The evidence-based secondary transition practices developed by Test, Fowler, et al. (2009a) also serve as a call for future research. First, future studies need to meet the quality indicators for group and/or single-subject research. The low number of practices is a direct result of the lack of high-quality research studies. For example, many transition-related skills (e.g., physical fitness, travel, managing finances, healthy living) do not have any evidence base. Second, although high-quality research is needed in all taxonomy categories, experimental research in family involvement and interagency collaboration are critically important. Finally, research is needed that links evidence-based instructional practices with improved post-school outcomes such as employment, education, and quality of life.

Among the 16 predicators of post-school success, the four that have evidence of success in all three areas of education, employment, and independent living are inclusion in general education, paid work experience, self-care/independent living, and student support. More research is needed in the other categories.

OVERVIEW OF THIS BOOK

The purpose of this book is to provide practitioners with a single source of information on evidence-based practices for teaching secondary transition skills to students with disabilities. This chapter provided a rationale for using transition-focused education and the Taxonomy for Transition Programming as frameworks for organizing evidence-based secondary transition practices. Chapter 2 provides specific strategies for collecting transition assessment data to develop IEPs and related transition services and instruction. Next, Chapter 3 describes simple strategies that can be used for teaching transition skills. Chapter 4 describes useful methods for collecting data to measure how well students are learning the

Table 1.3. Evidence-based in-school predictors of post-school success

Predictor/outcome	Education	Employment	Independent living
Career awareness	X	X	
Community experiences		X	
Exit examination requirements/ high school diploma status		X	
Inclusion in general education	X	X	X
Interagency collaboration	X	X	
Occupational courses	X	X	
Paid employment/work experience	X	X	X
Parental involvement		X	
Program of study		X	
Self-advocacy/self-determination	X	X	
Self-care/independent living	X	X	X
Social skills	X	X	
Student support	X	X	X
Transition program	X	X	
Vocational education	X	X	
Work study		X	

secondary transition skills they are being taught. The remaining chapters provide readers with descriptions of evidence-based practices in the areas of student-focused planning (Chapter 5), employment skills (Chapter 6), life skills (Chapter 7), and academic skills (Chapter 8). Chapters 5–8 also contain example practice descriptions and research-to-practice lesson plan starters. Because it is impossible to write lesson plans that meet the requirements of every state and local education, research-to-practice lesson plan starters provide teachers with basic information needed to develop a lesson plan including an objective, setting and materials, content to be taught, teaching procedures, and an evaluation strategy. All material in the research-to-practice lesson plan starters was taken directly from one of the published articles used by Test, Fowler, et al. (2009a) to establish the evidence base for the practice. As a result, practitioners will have access to information that can help them assess a student's secondary transition needs, develop IEP instructional goals and objectives, design and implement evidence-based lesson plans, and assess the effects of their instruction.

FOR FURTHER INFORMATION

SPP/APR Indicators

National Dropout Prevention Center for Students with Disabilities (http://www.dropout prevention.org)

This federally funded technical assistance center is charged with helping states improve their graduation and dropout rates.

National Secondary Transition Technical Assistance Center (http://www.nsttac.org)

This federally funded technical assistance center is charged with helping states improve the transition component of student IEPs.

National Post-School Outcomes Center (http://www.psocenter.org)

This federally funded technical assistance center is charged with helping states improve the data collection system used to collect post-school outcomes on students with disabilities.

Post-School Outcomes

National Longitudinal Transition Survey 2 (http://www.nlts2.org)

This web site contains the reports from a 10-year study of the post-school outcomes of 12,000 youth nationwide who were ages 13–16 in 2000. Information was collected from parents, youth, and schools to provide a national picture of experiences and achievements of young people as they transitioned into early adulthood.

Evidence-Based Practices

Cook, B.G., Tankersley, M., Cook, L., & Landrum, T.J. (2008). Evidence-based practices in special education: Some practical considerations. *Intervention in School and Clinic, 44*(2), 69–75.

Explains evidence-based practices and how they are determined.

Aligning Transition and Standards-Based Education

Kochhar-Bryant, C.A., & Bassett, D.S. (2002). Challenge and promise in aligning transition and standards-based education. In C.A. Kochhar-Bryant & D.S. Bassett (Eds.), *Aligning transition and standards-based education: Issues and strategies* (pp. 1–24). Arlington, VA: Council for Exceptional Children.

This text provides the basic context for standards-based education and provides strategies for how to align secondary transition with standards-based education.

2

Transition Assessment for Instruction

Dawn A. Rowe, Larry Kortering, and David W. Test

Transition assessment is included in the student development category of the Taxonomy for Transition Programming (Kohler, 1996), which focuses on identifying the strengths and needs of students with disabilities in the area of secondary transition. Transition assessment is a specific subcategory of student development that includes both curriculum-based and situational vocational assessment, as well as academic, cognitive, and adaptive behavior assessments. Two case studies, Luke and Jacqueline, are discussed in this chapter to show how transition assessment can be used to write postsecondary goals, choose appropriate transition assessments, write annual individualized education program (IEP) goals to support postsecondary goals, and design instruction for students with disabilities in secondary transition.

 **LUKE**

Luke is a 16-year-old boy with a specific learning disability in reading and reading comprehension. He attends a neighborhood high school as a sophomore. He is an attentive student and active member of his school and community. Luke is currently the treasurer of the student council and plays racquetball in a community league with some of his friends. He also participates regularly in activities with the youth group at his church. In his free time, he enjoys watching sports (e.g., basketball, hockey, football) on television or in person. He has a part-time summer job with a local grocery store and is saving money to purchase a car. He has been able to successfully juggle his recreational activities while completing all his schoolwork on time and having a nearly perfect attendance record. Luke's post-school plans are to work in the hospitality and tourism field.

 JACQUELINE

Jacqueline is an 18-year-old young woman with severe multiple cognitive and physical disabilities. She attends her neighborhood high school as a senior; however, she will remain in high school until she ages out at 21 years old. Jacqueline participates in some social and academic activities planned by the school with her same-age peers without disabilities. At home, her parents report that she enjoys watching television and listening to audio books or music. She does not participate in community activities outside of school. Jacqueline's family plans for her to attend an adult day center to continue her education and training after high school.

Luke and Jacqueline need transition-rich IEPs to prepare them for their future post-secondary endeavors. A transition-rich IEP starts with transition assessment and a statement of present levels of performance. By conducting transition assessments and writing thorough present levels of performance, the other components of a transition-rich IEP will fall into place (see Figure 2.1).

TRANSITION ASSESSMENTS: THE KEY TO A TRANSITION-RICH INDIVIDUALIZED EDUCATION PROGRAM

A transition-rich IEP is a product of thorough and ongoing transition assessment leading to appropriate postsecondary goals, transition services, and annual IEP goals. It is the starting point in the transition planning process (see Figure 2.2). Transition assessment is critical to developing a transition-rich IEP because it is the first step in identifying current levels of performance, writing measurable postsecondary goals, identifying appropriate transition services, and developing annual IEP goals to support the attainment of a student's postsecondary goals.

The ultimate goal of transition assessment is to foster self-understanding while helping students make informed choices, take charge of the transition process, and understand the skills needed for post-school environments. The following are some guiding questions

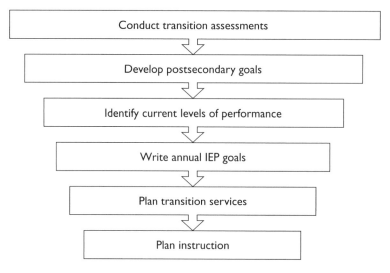

Figure 2.1. Steps in the transition planning process. (*Source:* Mazzotti et al., 2009. *Key:* IEP, individualized education program.)

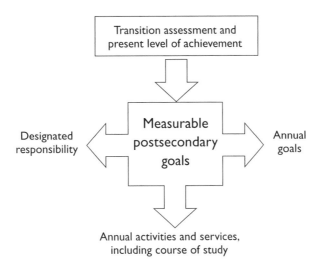

Figure 2.2. Transition-rich individualized education program. (From Mazzotti, V. [2007, January]. *Transition-rich IEPs*. Ft. Worth, TX; reprinted by permission.)

to consider when choosing and conducting transition assessments (Colorado Department of Education, 2001):

1. Where is the individual presently?

2. Where is the individual going?

3. How do we get the individual there?

DEFINITION AND TYPES OF TRANSITION ASSESSMENT

Sitlington, Neubert, and Leconte (1997) defined transition assessment as an ongoing process of collecting information on a student's strengths, preferences, interests, and needs as they relate to future learning, living, and working environments. Transition assessment is a broad concept spanning all areas relating to the transition from school to adulthood, including career and vocational assessment, academic assessment, community adjustment, and independent living. Past laws and corresponding reauthorizations that facilitate transition assessment include the Rehabilitation Act Amendments of 1992 (PL 102-569), Individuals with Disabilities Education Act (IDEA) of 1990 (PL 101-476), Carl D. Perkins Vocational and Applied Technology Act Amendments of 1990 (PL 101-392), Job Training Reform Amendments of 1992 (PL 102-367), and the School-to-Work Opportunities Act of 1994 (PL 103-239).

Individuals with Disabilities Education Improvement Act of 2004 (PL 108-446) required that beginning no later than age 16, all students have IEPs that include coordinated, measurable annual goals and transition services that will reasonably enable them to attain their postsecondary goals. To meet this requirement, educators must begin the transition assessment process of collecting information about an individual's strengths, preferences, interests, and needs as they relate to the demands of current and future working, educational, living, and personal and social environments.

Primary assessment areas can include interests, preferences, cognitive development, academic performance, adaptive behavior, interpersonal relationship skills, emotional and

mental health development, general and specific employability skills, and community participation
(Sitlington & Clark, 2007). In addition, areas such as
daily attendance record, performance on high-stakes
assessments (e.g., end-of-course examinations, com-
petency examinations), work- or training-based performance measures, and related indices provide useful
information.

*Beginning no later than the first IEP
(when the child turns 16, or younger if
determined appropriate by the IEP
team) and updated annually thereafter,
the IEP must include appropriate measurable postsecondary goals based
upon age-appropriate transition assessments related to training, education,
employment, and (where appropriate)
independent living skills (IDEA, 2004).*

Although transition assessment first provides a
foundation of information that sets the stage for the
transition planning process, it is recommended that assessment data be collected on an ongoing basis with
an interdisciplinary team approach using formal and
informal assessments to identify students' strengths, needs, and preferences (Neubert,
2003). In fact, it has been suggested that students begin developing a worker identity
and general understanding of the work world as early as elementary school (Porfeli, Hartung, & Vondracek, 2008); however, many states choose to begin at age 16, when the
federal law requires transition planning.

Beginning the assessment process early allows time for students to develop an understanding of who they are and what they want in life. In middle school, transition assessment starts the process of helping students understand their interests and talents while ex-
periencing the importance of general employability skills (e.g., attendance, punctuality,
responsibility). This is an evolving process that helps students refine their interests and preferences, gain awareness of job and community activities, determine accommodations and
support needs, and develop tentative postsecondary goals. In high school, transition assessment sets the stage for students to further refine their interests and preferences and explore potential work, postsecondary education, and independent living environments. At
the same time, students can identify appropriate courses to take, as well as employment
experiences to help them develop the necessary skill sets to attain their goals. These skill
sets should include the development of specific employability skills or skills that relate to
a specific career.

Assessment information also can assist students in articulating individual needs, preferences, and interests to employers, instructors at postsecondary education institutions,
and personnel in community or adult service agencies. As students approach school completion, assessment data also helps adult service providers in planning and providing appropriate support services beyond high school (Clark, 1996; Levinson, 1994). Transition assessments typically involve both formal and informal assessment.

Formal Assessments

Formal assessments are standardized instruments that have been tested for reliability and
validity to support their use (Walker, Fowler, Kortering, & Rowe, 2010). One advantage
of formal assessments is having a norm (i.e., comparison) group along with a technical
manual. For example, in the case of aptitude or interest testing, having a norm group allows comparison of a given student's performance or measured interests to that of a peer
group, which represents the general population or specific subgroup that the student
might be competing against for a given job. For instance, a student who expresses an in-

terest in mechanical careers (e.g., construction, carpentry) can be evaluated to see how his or her mechanical aptitude for such a job compares to samples from a community college, technical training program, or mechanical occupation. In addition, a technical manual can provide users with information on an assessment's development, recommended uses, and supporting materials. This information can help in evaluating the overall quality of the instrument.

Some of the more popular formal interest assessments or inventories include the Harrington-O'Shea Career Decision Making System (Harrington & O'Shea, 2000), Kuder Career Planning System (Luzzo, Rottinghaus, & Zytowski, 2006), Self-Directed Search (Holland, 1994, 1996; Holland & Powell, 1994), and Wide Range Interest and Occupation Test (Glutting & Wilkinson, 2003). Other types of formal assessments include academic achievement tests such as the Woodcock-Johnson III Tests of Achievement (Woodcock, McGrew, & Mather, 2000); adaptive behavior scales including the Vineland Adaptive Behavior Scales (Sparrow, Cicchetti, & Balla, 2005); and general or specific aptitude tests represented by the Occupational Aptitude Survey and Interest Schedule (Parker, 2002), Armed Services Vocational Aptitude Battery (U.S. Department of Defense, 2005), Bennett Mechanical Comprehension Test (Bennett, 2006), and Wiesen Test of Mechanical Comprehension (Wiesen, 1997). Other formal tests provide information relative to a student's personality, such as the Myers-Briggs Type Indicator (Myers & Briggs, 1988); a student's ability to adjust to work, such as the Work Adjustment Scale (Gilliam, 1994); and general or specific work performance measures, such as Becker's Work Adjustment Profile (Becker, 2000), the Job Observation and Behavior Scale (Rosenburg & Brady, 2000), the Job Search Attitude Survey (Liptak, 2006), and the Work Personality Profile (Neath & Bolton, 2008).

Informal Assessments

Informal assessments are more subjective and require multiple administrations by various observers to strengthen the validity of the measure. Informal assessments include paper-and-pencil tests, observations, interviews, environmental analysis, and curriculum-based assessments (Walker et al., 2010). A major advantage of informal assessments is that they are often inexpensive and easy to use; some measures are even available online, such as the Ansell-Casey Life Skills Assessment (Ansell & Casey Family Programs, 2009) and iTransition (Postsecondary Education Programs Network, 2008).

Examples of paper-and-pencil informal assessments include the Transition Planning Inventory–Revised (Clark & Patton, 2009), Enderlee-Severson Transition Rating Scales (Enderlee & Severson, 2003), the Life-Centered Career Education Performance and Knowledge Battery (Brolin, 2004), and the Transition Behavior Scale (McCarney & Anderson, 2000). Other valuable methods of informal vocational or independent living assessment include observing a student in various employment-related situations (Clark, Patton, & Moulton, 2000), talking with a student about likes and dislikes, and providing opportunities to experience various community activities and events (Sitlington & Payne, 2004; Synatschk, Clark, & Patton, 2008). Academic and transition skills may also be assessed using curriculum-based assessments such as task analysis, portfolio assessment, work sample analysis, and criterion-referenced tests (Roessler, 2000; Sitlington & Clark, 2007). A final area of informal assessment involves complete criterion-referenced curricula and assessment packages, such as the Brigance Transition Skills Inventory (Curriculum Associates, 2010).

 **LUKE**

Luke's Assessments

Luke was administered several formal assessments from seventh to 10th grade. He was administered a full battery of psychological assessments, including the Wechsler Intelligence Scale for Children (Wechsler, 2004) and the Test of Academic Achievement Skills (Gardner, 1989). Results of these assessments indicated that Luke had an overall full-scale IQ of 115. Although his academic levels were on par with his IQ in the areas of written language and math, his oral reading and reading comprehension were well below expected levels, which qualified him for a specific learning disability in reading and reading comprehension. Luke also demonstrated below-average reading skills, based on the Woodcock-Johnson III Tests of Achievement (Woodcock et al., 2000). His written language and math skills were somewhat above average. He successfully passed all the necessary academic classes and end-of-course examinations for the 10th grade. Results of the Self-Directed Search (Holland, 1994) indicated that Luke should consider careers that are social, artistic, and enterprising, which matched his aspirations of hospitality and tourism.

Luke also participated in several informal assessments including interviews, interest inventories, and transition planning inventories. Results of these assessments indicated that Luke had excellent attendance throughout high school and was on track to earn a standard high school diploma. His special education case manager noted Luke's interest in the hospitality and tourism industry, which was supported by his parents. On the O*NET Career Interest Inventory (U.S. Department of Labor, 2001), Luke's highest interest areas were social and enterprising. Given his previous work history, he also took the Work Adjustment Inventory (Gilliam, 1994), on which he scored high on the activity, empathy, and adaptability scales and low on assertiveness. This score pattern suggests a preference for an active job that provides regular changes in work routines and settings, as well as coworkers who can appreciate Luke's empathy for others. However, Luke's low score on the assertiveness scale suggested that he may have difficulty asserting himself in some work and personal situations. When completing the Transition Planning Inventory (Clark & Patton, 2009), Luke identified specific transition-related needs in the area of planning for further education and training. Specifically, he was concerned by not knowing how to gain entry into the college or university of his choice and how to succeed in an appropriate postsecondary program.

 **JACQUELINE**

Jacqueline's Assessments

Jacqueline also participated in an extensive ongoing assessment process that included formal and informal assessments. Jacqueline's intense medical needs required assessments from medical doctors and other related service providers in addition to teachers and family members. Reports from medical doctors state that Jacqueline requires daily assistance from a nurse because of a number of significant medical issues (e.g., tracheotomy, use of a ventilator, feeding through a gastrostomy tube). Jacqueline also has a severe seizure disorder, which has resulted in a dependence on medication and 24-hour supervision. A speech evaluation found that Jacqueline uses facial gestures to communicate her likes and dislikes, such as a smile to show contentment and a blank stare to indicate disinterest. She uses simple one-button communication devices with assistance when offered during class activities. Jacqueline relies on a manual wheelchair to navigate her surroundings, but requires assistance to maneuver her wheelchair in and out of classrooms and in small spaces. She is able to push her chair using one hand but takes a long time to travel any distance. She requires a two-person lift or mechanical device for all transfers, as well as hand-over-hand assistance for all activities because of her limited fine motor skills. She is dependent on a personal care attendant for tasks such as toileting, teeth brushing, and hair combing. Results of the Supports Intensity Scale (Thompson et al., 2004) indicated that Jacqueline requires full physical assistance hourly for most of the day for all life activities. It also indicated that she has a high prevalence of medical support needs (e.g., suctioning of tracheotomy, tube feeding, turning and positioning, seizure management).

Structured interviews with the family and classroom observations indicated Jacqueline is inquisitive. She stays awake and alert throughout most of the school day and seems to always want to be a part of conversations around her. She enjoys receiving verbal and tactile attention from her peers and teachers. She is tolerant of position changes on a mat table and allows hand-over-hand assistance to participate in activities. She is also able to activate a variety of devices (e.g., radio, computer) using a switch with assistance. Jacqueline completed the YES (Your Employment Selections) employment selection survey (http://yesjobsearch.com; Morgan, Morgan, Despain, & Vasquez, 2006) to determine some occupational interest. The survey revealed that she prefers jobs that involve working with or being around people, as well as a quieter working environment that is bright and spacious. Results of the family transition interview indicated that Jacqueline's parents will need assistance providing ongoing 24-hour support for her medical and personal needs. The family also preferred that Jacqueline continue her daily routine of going somewhere outside the home to interact with others and participate in activities in the community.

USING TRANSITION ASSESSMENT TO WRITE POSTSECONDARY GOALS

Transition assessment helps students to identify their postsecondary goals. Informal and formal assessments can be used to determine what type of postsecondary education or employment a student is interested in, where and with whom they want to live after high school, what type of supports they will need to achieve these goals, and what skills they will need to be successful. Identifying postsecondary goals is essential to developing a transition component that reflects a student's interests and needs (Sitlington, 2008; Sitlington & Clark, 2001).

The assessment data for Luke provides clear and relevant information needed to plan for his current and future education, training, and employment. The informal interviews with Luke and his family suggested that he wants to pursue a career in the hospitality and tourism industry; the results of the interest inventories further validated this aspiration. From this information, the IEP team can develop a measurable postsecondary goal in employment; for example, the goal may state the following: *After graduation from high school, Luke will obtain an entry-level job in the hospitality and tourism industry.* As Luke moves closer to graduation from high school and learns more about the industry, this goal should become more refined based on his interests, preferences, and needs: *After obtaining his degree from the university, Luke will work as a public relations specialist for a major hotel chain.*

The IEP team can also develop a postsecondary goal in education and training with this assessment information. When Luke explored this career options, he discovered that most of the positions required a bachelor's degree, although there were some positions requiring an associate's degree. Therefore, because Luke will need to continue his education after high school, his postsecondary goal on an early IEP may state the following: *After graduation from high school, Luke will attend a 4-year university.* Again, as Luke gets closer to high school graduation, his goal can become more specific: *After graduation from high school, Luke will attend Johnson & Wales University and major in Travel, Tourism, and Hospitality Management.*

Jacqueline's assessment information suggests that a less traditional route to postsecondary education and training, employment, and independent living will be necessary. The family transition assessment revealed a need for 24-hour support and continued interaction with peers after high school. Results of her interest inventory indicated that Jacqueline would prefer to work in a place that is quiet where she would have the opportunity to interact with others. By taking into consideration all assessment data, the IEP team can formulate a measurable postsecondary goal for employment: *After exiting high school, Jacqueline will obtain a trainee position at the occupational training center.* As Jacqueline moves closer to exiting high school and acquires more skills, her postsecondary goal may be revised based on her interests, preferences, and needs: *After exiting high school, Jacqueline will participate in customized employment at the local library with ongoing supports from the community rehabilitation program.*

Jacqueline's IEP team has enough information to develop a postsecondary education and training goal for Jacqueline. Based on observations and interviews with families and other stakeholders, Jacqueline will need continued training in basic daily living skills, community skills, and social integration. Therefore, an appropriate postsecondary goal in education and training may state the following: *After graduation, Jacqueline will participate in a center-based program that provides training in daily living skills along with community and social integration.* By the time she is ready to leave high school, supports may be in place for her to transition into a specific facility, or she may need to focus on more specific skills to be successful in that environment. Therefore, this goal may also be further developed as she gets closer to exiting high school: *After exiting high school, Jacqueline will participate in functional skill training through the community alternatives program four times per week at the center-based program and in the community to develop her functional communication skills.*

The other area that will need to be addressed for Jacqueline is independent living. Because of the nature and severity of Jacqueline's disability, it will be necessary for her IEP team to write a measurable postsecondary goal in independent living: *After exiting high school, Jacqueline will use an augmentative communication device at home and the center-based program to communicate her wants, needs, and desires and to independently interact with her environment.*

USING TRANSITION ASSESSMENT TO WRITE PRESENT LEVELS OF PERFORMANCE

Another important use of transition assessment information is developing the present level of academic and functional performance in the IEP. Present levels of academic and functional performance are directly linked to other components of the IEP (Bateman & Herr, 2006). For example, if a statement of present levels of performance (PLOP) describes a problem with a student's reading level and points to a specific reading skill such as comprehension, this should be addressed in the annual IEP goals and possibly transition services.

The PLOP is the starting point for writing annual IEP goals that support the attainment of postsecondary goals. The PLOP should answer the question, "What does a student need to learn or need to do better?" By examining transition assessment information, one can determine the starting point from which the year's progress in academic and functional behavior can be measured (Bateman & Herr, 2006).

In terms of academic performance, Luke's PLOP may state the following:

> Results of the Wechsler Intelligence Scale for Children (Wechsler, 2004) and the Test of Academic Achievement Skills (Gardner, 1989) indicated that Luke's academic levels were on par with his IQ in the areas of written language and math; however, his oral reading and reading comprehension skills are well below expected levels. Results of the Woodcock-Johnson Tests of Achievement (Woodcock et al., 2000) also indicated Luke demonstrated above-average written language and math skills but below-average reading skills.

In terms of functional performance, Luke's PLOP may state the following:

> The Work Adjustment Inventory (Gilliam, 1994) indicated high scores for activity, empathy, and adaptability, suggesting a preference for jobs that keep Luke active, allow him to work with coworkers who appreciate his empathy for others, and offer changes in work routines and settings. He scored low on assertiveness, suggesting that he may have difficulty asserting himself in some work and personal situations.

In terms of academic performance, Jacqueline's PLOP may state the following:

> Jacqueline uses facial expressions (e.g., smile, blank stare) to communicate her likes and dislikes. She is able to activate a switch with assistance to engage in a variety of activities and to communicate with her teachers and peers.

In terms of functional performance, Jacqueline's PLOP may state the following:

> Results of the family transition interview and the Supports Intensity Scale (Thompson et al., 2004) suggested Jacqueline needs intense support for her medical and personal needs; however, Jacqueline and her family desire that she participate in these activities to the maximum extent possible.

USING TRANSITION ASSESSMENT TO WRITE ANNUAL INDIVIDUALIZED EDUCATION PROGRAM GOALS

Transition assessment is also valuable when determining appropriate annual IEP goals that will support a student's attainment of their postsecondary goals. For each postsecondary goal, there must be at least one annual IEP goal that will help the student make progress and stay on track for a successful transition. Some questions to consider would be the following (Walker et al., 2010).

1. To achieve the identified postsecondary goals, what skills and knowledge must the student attain this academic year?

2. What skills and knowledge does the student currently possess to support these postsecondary goals?

Consider Luke's postsecondary goal of employment. After graduation from high school, Luke will obtain a job in the hospitality and tourism industry. The IEP team knows that he should begin to explore the hospitality and tourism industry this year to understand the necessary requirements to enter the field and eventually narrow his choice of jobs within the field. Based on his transition assessment information and PLOP, the IEP team knows that Luke will need to continue working on his reading and reading comprehension skills. Therefore, the team should consider the role of learning strategies, assistive technology, and accommodations. In addition, according to the Work Adjustment Inventory, Luke needs to develop his interpersonal skills, particularly assertiveness. These results may lead the IEP team to develop an annual IEP goal related to increasing Luke's interpersonal skills. For example, the goal may state: *Given direct instruction, modeling, and opportunities to interact in social and work situations, Luke will express his beliefs, feelings, or opinions using an "I want" or "I feel" statement three out of four times by the end of the fall semester of school.*

For Luke's postsecondary goal of education or training (i.e., attending a 4-year university), the IEP team knows that Luke will require sufficient academic skills in reading, writing, and math to obtain this goal. Based on the transition assessment information and Luke's PLOP reported earlier, Luke will continue to need support in reading and reading comprehension. Therefore, the team may construct an annual IEP goal to increase Luke's reading ability and comprehension skills, such as the following: *Given a story map and short story, Luke will identify the components of a story (i.e., characters, setting, and problem) with 90% accuracy.*

These are just a few examples of IEP goals that would support Luke's postsecondary goals in education and employment, based on transition assessment information and his PLOP. It is important that the IEP team carefully analyze all assessment data to determine appropriate goals to assist students in the acquisition of their postsecondary aspirations.

Jacqueline should also have at least one annual goal to support each of her postsecondary goals. Based on her transition assessment information, PLOP, and postsecondary goal in employment (i.e., obtaining a trainee position at the occupational training center), an appropriate annual goal may be the following: *Given multiple vocational tasks in the classroom, Jacqueline will increase her productivity by 10% as measured by time on task during a 20-minute training session during one school semester.*

Based on Jacqueline's transition assessment information, PLOP, and postsecondary goal in education and training (i.e., participating in a center-based program designed to teach daily living skills along with community and social integration), an appropriate annual goal could be the following: *Given a board displaying two choices of classroom and community topics (e.g., instructional activities, work-based instruction activities), Jacqueline will use a switch associated with each item to select the activity or item in which she wants to engage with 80% accuracy by December of the IEP school year.*

Based on transition assessment information and her PLOP, Jacqueline's postsecondary goal for independent living was to use an augmentative communication device at home and the center-based program to communicate her wants, needs, and desires and to interact with her environment more independently. Jacqueline can begin acquiring the skills necessary to operate an augmentative device by mastering the following annual IEP goal: *Given daily opportunities for choice making, and a verbal prompt, Jacqueline will use a switch to express her preference on 80% of occasions for the duration of the IEP.*

It is important for the IEP team to consider all transition assessment information when determining what skills will be needed to obtain postsecondary goals, what skills a student already possesses, and what skills need to be developed or refined for a student to progress toward these postsecondary goals.

USING TRANSITION ASSESSMENT
TO DETERMINE TRANSITION SERVICES

Once an IEP team has established postsecondary goals, PLOP, and annual IEP goals, the team should develop needed transition services. To accomplish this task, the IEP team needs to identify transition services that provide students with the practical and experiential skills and knowledge that will assist in a successful transition. According to IDEA 2004, there are several areas in which transition services can be provided, including instruction related to academic success; related services such as vocational rehabilitation, community experiences related to employment or education, and acquisition of daily living and independent living skills; and functional vocational evaluation. When trying to determine appropriate transition services, the IEP team should consider the following questions (Walker et al., 2010):

1. What particular skills and knowledge does the student already have in each of the areas of education and training, employment, and independent living?

2. What knowledge and skills does the student still need to acquire to obtain these goals in education and training, employment, and independent living?

The answers to these questions will be critical in determining appropriate transition services for a student and in planning for a successful transition. In particular, the IEP should address the areas in which the student most needs to increase his or her knowledge and skills to prepare for the transition to adulthood.

For Luke, transition services might include the following:

*   Instruction related to hospitality and tourism (e.g., hospitality course elective at a local community college)
*   Strategies to help him be academically successful
*   Assistance with college entrance examinations and accommodation requests
*   Self-determination instruction
*   Interviews with individuals in the hospitality and tourism industry
*   Visits to universities and their disability resource centers

All of these transition services will support Luke's aspirations of attending a 4-year university and becoming a public relations specialist.

Jacqueline's transition services might include self-care instruction, community-based independent and community living instruction, speech and occupational therapy for augmentative communication evaluation, and selecting an appropriate augmentative communication device for use in school and post-school environments. She will also need nursing services. Other appropriate transition services for Jacqueline may include tours of recreational agencies/facilities in the community and adult day programs, assistance

Transition services are designed to be within a results-oriented process. This process should be focused on improving the academic and functional achievement of the child with a disability to facilitate the child's movement from school to post-school activities. It should be based on the individual child's needs, taking into account the child's strengths, preferences, and interests (IDEA, 2004).

with disability management, and help applying for Social Security assistance. All of these transition services will support her postsecondary education and training, employment, and independent-living goals. Taken together, the resulting transition services will allow Luke,

Jacqueline, and their families to explore, plan, and construct a useful and practical bridge to the adult world.

USING TRANSITION ASSESSMENT TO GUIDE INSTRUCTION

Finally, transition assessment should guide instruction in terms of what skills to teach and how to best teach those skills. It should also be used to determine courses and related experiences a student will need to complete in high school to support postsecondary goals.

In terms of skill development, three considerations are relevant. First, the transition assessment information provides insight into existing skills, possible talents, and limitations. This information must be considered against a backdrop of what it will take, in terms of skills, to help students graduate and be prepared for future success in a chosen career. The former may be dictated by state and local graduation requirements. These requirements may warrant specific skill instruction or remediation (e.g., improving reading or math skills), supplementary learning experiences or support (e.g., online learning opportunities), and academic support (e.g., after-school support). Career requirements are readily available through sites sponsored by the U.S. Department of Labor (http://www.oneton line.org/) and U.S. Bureau of Labor Statistics (http://www.bls.gov).

Second, transition assessment information can also be used to modify instruction as needed to help the student be as successful as possible. For example, a student who demonstrated interest and talent in mechanical aptitude or skills could be motivated to succeed in a geometry class by having the teacher link algebraic content to mechanical fields (e.g., using carpentry as vehicle to teach the concept of area and perimeter).

The third consideration is related to courses. The information from transition assessment should help students identify a course of study, including electives that will best prepare them for their postsecondary goals. These courses may be influenced by a student's postsecondary education or training goals (e.g., career technical course of study, university preparation) and employment. Finally, the information may help identify appropriate summer employment and community experiences (Carter et al., 2010), after-school or weekend experiences including paid jobs and volunteer or service opportunities, and related job or career experiences (Lapan, 2004).

Instruction for Luke and Jacqueline should be guided by their present levels of academic and functional performance and annual IEP goals. Daily progress monitoring through formal and informal transition assessments can guide instruction on specific skills. For example, one of Luke's annual IEP goals is to identify the components of a story (i.e., characters, setting, and problem) with 90% accuracy when given a story map and short story. Using curriculum-based measurements such as AIMSweb Pro Reading (PsychCorp, 2010), a teacher can monitor progress and adjust instruction based on results. If Luke continues to show deficits in identifying the components of a story based on the assessment information, the teacher may choose to change the instructional method (e.g., explicit one-to-one instruction as opposed to small group), modify the assignment, or provide an accommodation such as read aloud.

One of Jacqueline's IEP goals is to use a switch to express her preference on 80% of occasions when given daily opportunities for choice making and a verbal prompt. In this case, the teacher might alter instruction by fading the prompt and possibly adding more items from which to choose. The teacher may also adjust the mastery criteria from 80% to 90% or 100%.

Transition assessment is an ongoing process that guides the development of postsecondary goals, PLOP, annual IEP goals, transition services, and instruction (see Figure 2.1). By using this process, educators will be prepared to meet the requirements of Indicator 13.

TRANSITION ASSESSMENT AND INDICATOR 13

To ensure states were meeting the guidelines of IDEA 2004, the Office of Special Education Programs (OSEP) began requiring states to submit data on 20 indicators for Part B (i.e., children with disabilities ages 3–22; U.S. Department of Education OSEP, 2009). Indicator 13 is the secondary transition indicator and requires that the IEP include

> Appropriate measurable postsecondary goals that are annually updated and based upon an age appropriate transition assessment, transition services, and courses of study that will reasonably enable the student to meet their postsecondary goals. There also must be evidence that the student was invited to the IEP Team meeting where transition services were discussed and evidence that, if appropriate, a representative of any participating agency was invited to the IEP Team meeting with the prior consent of the parent or student who has reached the age of majority (20 U.S.C. 1416[a][3][B]; U.S. Department of Education OSEP, 2009).

To help educators meet annual data reporting requirements, the National Secondary Transition Technical Assistance Center (NSTTAC), in coordination with OSEP, developed an Indicator 13 checklist (see Figure 2.3; NSTTAC, 2009). The checklist includes eight items related to transition for students with disabilities. Six components of the checklist are related to using transition assessment data to guide writing measurable postsecondary goals and then aligning postsecondary goals with transition services and annual IEP goals:

1. Is (are) there an appropriate measurable postsecondary goal or goals in this area (i.e., employment, education/training, and (if applicable) independent living)?

2. Is (are) the postsecondary goal(s) updated annually?

3. Is there evidence that the measurable postsecondary goal(s) were based on an age-appropriate transition assessment?

4. Are there transition services in the IEP that will reasonably enable the student to meet his or her postsecondary goal(s)?

5. Do the transition services include courses of study that will reasonably enable the student to meet his or her postsecondary goal(s)?

6. Is (are) there annual IEP goal(s) related to the student's transition services needs?

If age-appropriate transition assessments are collected on an ongoing basis and used to drive the IEP decision-making process, this will result in a transition-rich IEP that is in compliance with six of the components of Indicator 13.

SUMMARY

Transition assessment is a process that should begin as early as middle school and continue through high school (Neubert, 2003; Sitlington, 2008). The purpose is to guide the

Indicator 13
Checklist

Percent of youth with individualized education programs (IEPs) ages 16 and above with an IEP that includes appropriate measurable postsecondary goals that are annually updated and based upon an age-appropriate transition assessment, transition services, including courses of study, that will reasonably enable the student to meet those postsecondary goals, and annual IEP goals related to the student's transition services needs. There also must be evidence that the student was invited to the IEP team meeting where transition services are to be discussed and evidence that, if appropriate, a representative of any participating agency was invited to the IEP team meeting with the prior consent of the parent or student who has reached the age of majority (20 U.S.C. 1416[a][3][B]).

Questions	Postsecondary goals		
	Education/ training	Employment	Independent living
1. Is there an appropriate measurable postsecondary goal or goals in this area?	Y N	Y N	Y N N/A
Can the goal(s) be counted? Will the goal(s) occur *after* the student graduates from school? Based on the information available about this student, does (do) the postsecondary goal(s) seem appropriate for this student? • If *yes* to all three, then circle Y OR if a postsecondary goal(s) is (are) *not* stated, circle N.			
2. Is (are) the postsecondary goal(s) updated annually?	Y N	Y N	Y N N/A
Was (were) the postsecondary goal(s) addressed/updated in conjunction with the development of the current IEP? • If *yes*, then circle Y OR if the postsecondary goal(s) was (were) *not* updated with the current IEP, circle N.			
3. Is there evidence that the measurable postsecondary goal(s) were based on age-appropriate transition assessment?	Y N	Y N	Y N
Is the use of transition assessment(s) for the postsecondary goal(s) mentioned in the IEP or evident in the student's file? • If *yes*, then circle Y OR if *no*, then circle N.			
4. Are there transition services in the IEP that will reasonably enable the student to meet his or her postsecondary goal(s)?	Y N	Y N	Y N
Is a type of instruction, related service, community experience, or development of employment and other post-school adult living objectives, and if appropriate, acquisition of daily living skills, and provision of a functional vocational evaluation listed in association with meeting the postsecondary goal(s)? • If *yes*, then circle Y OR if *no*, then circle N.			

Figure 2.3.   The National Secondary Transition Technical Assistance Center's Indicator 13 checklist.   *(continued)*

From National Secondary Transition Technical Assistance Center. (2009). *Indicator 13 Checklist.*
Retrieved from http://www.nsttac.org/indicator13/ChecklistFormB.pdf

In *Evidence-Based Instructional Strategies for Transition* by David W. Test.
(2012, Paul H. Brookes Publishing Co., Inc.)

Questions	Education/ training	Employment	Independent living
		Postsecondary goals	
5. Do the transition services include courses of study that will reasonably enable the student to meet his or her postsecondary goal(s)?	Y N	Y N	Y N
Do the transition services include courses of study that align with the student's postsecondary goal(s)? • If *yes*, then circle Y OR if *no*, then circle N.			
6. Is (are) there annual IEP goal(s) related to the student's transition services needs?	Y N	Y N	Y N
Is (are) an annual goal(s) included in the IEP that is/are related to the student's transition services needs? • If *yes*, then circle Y OR if *no*, then circle N.			
7. Is there evidence that the student was invited to the IEP team meeting where transition services were discussed?	Y N	Y N	Y N
For the current year, is there documented evidence in the IEP or cumulative folder that the student was invited to attend the IEP team meeting? • If *yes*, then circle Y OR if *no*, then circle N.			
8. If appropriate, is there evidence that a representative of any participating agency was invited to the IEP team meeting with the prior consent of the parent or student who has reached the age of majority?	Y N N/A	Y N N/A	Y N N/A
For the current year, is there evidence in the IEP that representatives of any of the following agencies/ services were invited to participate in IEP development including but not limited to postsecondary education, vocational education, integrated employment (including supported employment), continuing and adult education, adult services, independent living or community participation for this postsecondary goal? Was consent obtained from the parent (or student, for a student the age of majority)? • If *yes* to both, then circle Y. • If no invitation is evident and a participating agency is likely to be responsible for providing or paying for transition services and there was consent to invite them to the IEP meeting, then circle N. • If it is too early to determine if the student will need outside agency involvement, or no agency is likely to provide or pay for transition services, circle N/A. • If parent or individual student consent (when appropriate) was not provided, circle N/A.			

Does the IEP meet the requirements of Indicator 13? (Circle one)
Yes (all *Ys* or *N/As* for each item [1–8] on the checklist included in the IEP are circled)   or
  No (one or more *Ns* circled)

From National Secondary Transition Technical Assistance Center. (2009). *Indicator 13 Checklist.*
Retrieved from http://www.nsttac.org/indicator13/ChecklistFormB.pdf

In *Evidence-Based Instructional Strategies for Transition* by David W. Test.
(2012, Paul H. Brookes Publishing Co., Inc.)

decision-making process for students and their families as they transition through high school into adulthood. The use of multiple types of assessment is necessary to create a clear picture of a student's interests and needs as they relate to postsecondary education, employment, and independent living. It is important that data are organized to be easily understood by students, parents, and other support personnel. Collaboration is key to making the transition process seamless. Students, families, adult service providers, and postsecondary institutions should all be included in the transition assessment and decision-making process (Sitlington & Clark, 2007; Sitlington & Payne, 2004).

FOR FURTHER INFORMATION

National Secondary Transition Technical Assistance Center (http://www.nsttac.org)

NSTTAC is a federally funded technical assistance center charged with assisting states in improving the transition component of student IEPs. They offer the following products and tools for transition assessment:

Transition Assessment Annotated Bibliography (http://www.nsttac.org/products_and_resources/TransitionAssessmentAnnotatedBibliography.aspx)

Transition Assessment Presenter Guide (http://www.nsttac.org/products_and_resources/PresenterGuides/TransitionAssessmentPresenterGuides/Default.aspx)

Transition Assessment Toolkit (http://www.nsttac.org/products_and_resources/tag.aspx)

Transition Coalition (http://transitioncoalition.org)

The Transition Coalition is located at the University of Kansas, Department of Special Education and provides online information, support, and professional development on secondary transition topics. They offer the following support and professional development for transition assessment:

Online Transition Assessment Training Module (http://transitioncoalition.org/transition/module_home.php)

Transition Assessment Reviews (http://transitioncoalition.org/transition/assessment_review/all.php)

3

......

Teaching Strategies

Sharon M. Richter, April L. Mustian, and David W. Test

Teachers can improve students' knowledge and skills in meaningful ways by selecting valuable instructional content and using effective teaching strategies. As they design instruction to best serve students, teachers encounter two major decisions: what to teach and how to teach it. For transition-age students with disabilities, these decisions are especially important given students' impending entry into adult life upon exit from public school services.

The information included in this chapter has strong connections to two areas in the Taxonomy for Transition Programming (Kohler, 1996). First, instructional content decisions should reflect the skills and knowledge identified in student development, such as life skills instruction, employment skills instruction, career and vocational curricula, and structured work experiences. Next, state and local education agencies that provide personnel with training and resources to facilitate successful transition to adult life among students with disabilities reflect a transition-focused program structure.

INSTRUCTIONAL CONTENT: FINDING BALANCE

The No Child Left Behind Act of 2001 (NCLB; PL 107-110) mandated that instructional content align with state academic content standards for all students, including students with disabilities, at each grade level. Regarding instructional content, NCLB mandated that states provide guidelines for specific academic content for each grade level from kindergarten to 12th grade. As a result, students with disabilities experienced a number of benefits, such as inclusion in state and local accountability measures. For the first time, local, state, and federal governments considered the performance of all students with disabilities on statewide and alternate assessments as one indicator of how a school system is performing overall. Additionally, students with disabilities are now taught age-appropriate content that may have otherwise been neglected (e.g., *The Diary of Anne Frank* for seventh graders) for skills that teachers deemed more important to students' development.

However, special educators who serve students with significant intellectual disabilities must recognize that this law did not intend to detail all instructional content provided to these students. To best serve students with significant disabilities, special educators should balance instructional content between federally mandated grade-level academic skills and essential content beyond the federal requirements that is crucial to independence and quality of life among students with significant intellectual disabilities (see Table 3.1). Examples of such content include the following:

1. Nonacademic content, such as social skills and dressing

2. Academic content that is present in the state academic content standards overall, but not at a particular student's chronological grade level, such as
money skills for a ninth grader

Special educators must make decisions regarding instructional content that reflects both federal mandates and students' individual needs for nonacademic skills and knowledge that are critical to independence and quality of life.

3. Content appropriate for transition-aged students
age 18–21, such as employability skills and travel
training, given that NCLB mandated instructional
content only for students up to 12th grade

COMMUNITY-BASED AND COMMUNITY-REFERENCED INSTRUCTION

One way to gauge success is to evaluate students' post-school abilities to appropriately use skills learned in their high school classes. Special educators must consider the settings in which their students will use skills and knowledge after graduation to support successful community participation, which is called community-referenced instruction. Community-referenced instruction is promoted by teaching skills in places where they would naturally be used, which is called community-based instruction (CBI).

Community-referenced instruction uses the surrounding community as a reference point to design instruction so that students are prepared with skills needed for current and subsequent community settings. Community-referenced instruction uses instructional content that is essential to students' success in community settings. Community-referenced instruction teaches skills such as visiting the doctor, using public transportation, withdrawing money from an automated teller machine (ATM), performing job duties safely, borrowing a book from the library, going to a sporting event, and purchasing groceries.

The Benefits

Many reasons support teaching community-referenced skills in the settings in which the skills are needed. CBI is an evidence-based practice that has been used to teach skills to students

Table 3.1.   Examples of essential instructional content beyond guidance of federal guidelines for grade-level academics

Student	Grade	Instructional need	Do federal guidelines inform decisions regarding content?	Why or why not?
Sarah, age 9	Third grade	Putting on clothing	No	Skill is not aligned with standards for any grade
Josiah, age 16	10th grade	Using dollar bills to make purchases	No	Money skills are included in first-grade standards rather than 10th-grade standards.
Tyree, age 19	Transition	Any content	No	No standards for transition-level content

with disabilities (Test et al., 2009a). Table 3.2 provides a brief overview of some of the evidence that supports the use of CBI. In natural settings, students are exposed to an array of materials and experiences that are naturally present in community settings, which eliminates the need for special materials designed by a teacher. In addition, by training in the community, teachers are facilitating students' application of skills in the settings in which they will be used.

By teaching in the community, teachers minimize the need for additional training to foster generalization, as these considerations are inherent to instruction provided in community settings.

The Challenges

CBI is effective in improving and maintaining functional skills needed for the postsecondary life of students with disabilities. However, planning and implementing CBI poses challenges that are not present in traditional classroom instruction (Wissick, Gardner, & Langone, 1999). When designing CBI, teachers should make plans for the following:

1. Transporting students to instructional sites (e.g., walking, school bus, public transportation)

2. Getting permission for students to regularly leave the school campus (e.g., school administrator permission, parent permission)

3. Finding financial resources for transportation and community services (e.g., to practice purchasing skills in the community through shopping at a grocery store, students will need money)

4. Scheduling both school and community sites (e.g., lunch periods, availability of transportation, extremely busy or slow times at a local store, occupational therapy)

In addition to logistics associated with planning CBI, teachers must also consider the setting to design instruction that is appropriate for the community. First, specially designed instruction should be planned with respect to the natural ratios of society. Second, teachers must use inconspicuous strategies and materials. The guiding rationale for both of these principles is as follows: Teachers must provide instruction with regard to the expectations and challenges naturally present in the community.

Natural Ratios

Teachers must not infringe upon the natural ratios of persons with disabilities to persons without disabilities typically present in the community for several reasons. First, although

Table 3.2. Research supporting the use of community-based instruction

Researchers	What was taught?	Where?
Ferguson and McDonnell (1991)	Grocery skills	Three different grocery stores
Berg et al. (1995)	Ordering a meal and purchasing items at a sandwich counter	Shopping mall, fast-food restaurant, a cookie stand at mall, and a deli counter at a grocery store
Souza and Kennedy (2003)	Social interactions in community settings	Training on a bus and in a cafeteria

large groups of individuals with disabilities are welcomed in society, overwhelming a CBI setting with individuals with disabilities results in an instructional setting that is flawed. To prepare students for experiences in which they are expected to perform skills, settings and materials should represent the expectations and challenges typically associated with the setting. Second, it would be extremely difficult to actually provide instruction to such a large group. Figure 3.1 summarizes a situation in which natural ratios are violated and potential consequences.

Selecting Appropriate Strategies and Materials

Teachers must identify what the "typical" experiences are for people without disabilities and use this as a reference point in designing instruction. In doing so, teachers should uphold four additional principles when selecting strategies and materials for CBI:

1. Teachers should take advantage of the teachable moments that are inherent in community teaching settings rather than diminishing the authenticity of the teaching situation by intervening and controlling unnecessarily.

2. Instruction should aim to improve the independence of a student via self-prompting and self-monitoring strategies.

3. Instruction should include items that will be available to students in postsecondary life.

4. Instruction should preserve the dignity and perceived competence of the student being trained, while not attracting the attention of the general public.

The situation:		
A teacher friend of yours suggests a plan for a total of 20 transition-age students with intellectual disabilities and six school staff members to go out to lunch together at a local restaurant. This plan will certainly violate the guiding principle of natural ratios.		
To mimic 'ty pical' community experiences	*Instead of...*	*Opt for...*
	20 students sitting at one large table in the restaurant or 10 student pairs each sitting with one school employee in the restaurant at one time	Going out to eat in smaller groups (e.g., three students and one staff) on different days or to different restaurants
Potential consequences		
Flaws to the instructional setting	After waiting on two tables of four students each, the waitress realizes that a few of the students had difficulty ordering food verbally. From this point on, the waitress asks all of the students to "touch" the picture of what they would like to eat on the menu in an attempt to be helpful. The expectations have changed: If one student with a disability was out to lunch with one friend, this level of assistance would not likely be provided.	
Flaws to the instruction provided	When three strangers involved in a lunch meeting sit at a nearby table, school staff members inadvertently shift priorities from teaching to maintaining quiet and order, given the large number of students present.	

Figure 3.1. The consequences of violating natural ratios.

SIMULATED INSTRUCTION

CBI is community referenced and takes place in the community, where the skill is typically performed. However, community-referenced instruction can also be implemented in simulated settings, such as the classroom. Simulated instruction is community referenced (i.e., based on the expectations of the community) but takes place in a noncommunity setting, usually a classroom. For example, paying for items is a skill needed in the community; therefore, it is a type of community-referenced instruction (i.e., the community serves as a reference for the content taught). Teaching payment skills in the classroom is considered simulated instruction. Conversely, teaching payment skills in the community is considered CBI.

The Benefits

Special educators should also recognize that simulated instruction is a valuable strategy to teach community-referenced skills for several reasons. First, research indicates that students with disabilities have acquired a number of skills via simulated instruction. Table 3.3 provides a brief overview of research that illustrates the positive impact of simulated instruction. Second, teachers are familiar with the instructional decisions associated with simulated instruction, given that simulated instruction can be done in most school settings at most times of day and can be implemented using strategies familiar to teachers, such as whole-group, small-group, and individualized instruction. Third, teachers can improve the efficiency (i.e., speed) with which students acquire skills by teaching needed skills frequently throughout the school day via massed trials or distributed trials. Conversely, in a community setting, the number of opportunities that occur naturally to practice a certain skill might be infrequent, slowing skill acquisition. Figure 3.2 illustrates efficiency related to both simulated instruction and CBI.

The Challenges

To design simulated instruction, teachers must attempt to imitate the setting in which students will use skills; however, developing experiences that actually expose students to the characteristics of the community setting is challenging. First, when using simulated instruction, teachers must create materials that are realistic but also reasonable to create in terms of cost, time, and skills. Second, situations occur in the natural setting that are unpredictable and therefore difficult to embed in simulated instruction. For example, when teaching students to use an ATM in the community, the presence of other ATM users or encountering a machine that is out of money are valuable teachable moments that are difficult to imitate in simulated instruction. Other examples of unpredictable teachable moments include fire drills, receiving the wrong bill at a restaurant, and a detour encountered during

Table 3.3.   Research supporting the use of simulated instruction

Researchers	What was taught?	How?
Montague (1988)	Social skills for employment	Scripted lessons
Mechling and Cronin (2006)	Ordering a meal at a fast-food restaurant	Video-based instruction
Alberto, Cihak, and Gama (2005)	Using a bank machine	Video-based instruction
Mechling, Gast, and Langone (2002)	Read grocery store words	Video-based instruction

The situation:
Via data collection, a teacher identified that a student is independently completing all skills associated with eating out in a restaurant (e.g., ordering a meal, requesting additional drinks or condiments if needed, paying for the bill), excluding leaving a tip.

Target skill: Leaving a tip at a restaurant		
Type of instruction	*How does it work?*	*What are the likely results?*
Community-based instruction	Taking the student to eat in a restaurant once per week to teach the skill	Student exposure to authentic community settings (positive result) Less efficient learning given one weekly opportunity to leave a tip (negative result)
Simulated instruction	Teaching the skill 10 times each day with varied bill amounts (e.g., $9.42, $15.12, $6.31, $36.01)	More efficient learning given 10 daily opportunities to practice (positive result) Lack of exposure to authentic community settings (negative result)

Figure 3.2. Community-based instruction versus simulated instruction.

a walk to work because of construction. The unpredictability that is common in natural settings provides opportunities for students to develop independence in responding to the authentic challenges of community settings but can be quite difficult for teachers to approximate. Figure 3.3 provides additional examples of materials and procedures designed to mimic those of community settings.

THE RECOMMENDATION: PAIR SIMULATED INSTRUCTION WITH COMMUNITY-BASED INSTRUCTION

Despite the obstacles that exist in designing and implementing both simulated instruction and CBI, skills for community participation are essential for students with disabilities. Instruction that combines both natural and simulated settings is effective in teaching skills

The situation:
Sarah can pay for items up to $20.00 using cash in the community. She recently opened a checking account at her local bank and received a bank card. She has memorized the personal identification number associated with the account but has had difficulty using the card to withdraw money and to make purchases.

Type of instruction: Simulated	
Instructional consideration	*Examples*
Materials	To teach students to use a bank card in the community, create a plywood replica of a bank machine (Shafer, Inge, & Hill, 1986).
Procedures	To teach student to purchase items in the community, use verbal and visual cues that mimic those typically provided by a cashier in the community (Colyer & Collins, 1996).

Figure 3.3. Preparing for simulated instruction.

for community participation to students with disabilities (Alberto, Cihak, & Gama, 2005).

The Benefits

CBI paired with simulated instruction is supported by a wealth of research. Table 3.4 provides a brief overview of research that supports the use of CBI paired with simulated instruction.

Recent research indicated that CBI paired with simulated instruction is more effective in comparison to either simulated instruction alone or CBI alone (Cihak, Alberto, Kessler, & Taber, 2004).

Using both simulated instruction paired with CBI diminishes the need for teachers to spend time and money creating materials to replace opportunities for learning in the community because students will have exposure to the materials in the community. In addition, using both methods reduces the probability that a teacher will not expose students to unpredictable situations that are important to students' skill development. Simulated instruction paired with CBI is a good solution, given barriers to teaching in community settings (e.g., transportation, permission, cost, schedule limitations), which may result in fewer instructional sessions and, consequently, slower learning among students. Finally, pairing the two types of instruction will allow teachers to instruct larger groups in the classroom and use instructional strategies that are most effective while maintaining natural ratios and using inconspicuous strategies and materials for community instruction. Figure 3.4 provides a weeklong plan for instruction that pairs simulated instruction and CBI.

The Challenges

With simulated instruction paired with CBI, most challenges can be alleviated by teaching skills in the two instructional settings. One important consideration is data collection for community participation skills. First, data should be collected during simulated instruction because this instruction is likely to occur daily (or at least a few times each week). Additionally, to gauge students' skill generalization, data must be collected in natural settings (Alberto et al., 2005; Mechling & Cronin, 2006). In other words, to gain information about students' abilities to use skills in settings where they are actually needed, data collection must take place in the CBI settings rather than only in the simulated settings. See Table 3.5 for guidance on collecting data in CBI settings.

SELECTING EVIDENCE-BASED INSTRUCTIONAL PRACTICES FOR SIMULATED INSTRUCTION AND COMMUNITY-BASED INSTRUCTION

Four recommendations are especially important when planning and implementing instruction aimed to improve community participation. First, using constant time delay

Table 3.4. Research supporting the use of community-based instruction paired with simulated instruction

Researchers	What was taught?	How?
Pattavina, Bergstrom, Marchand-Martella, and Martella (1992)	Safe street crossing	Simulated instruction included photos of streets and community-based instruction on public streets.
Taber, Alberto, Hughes, and Seltzer (2002)	Making cell phone calls when lost	Simulated instruction included learning skills in the classroom before additional practice in a grocery store, public library, and a department store.

Monday	Skill area: Bank machine skills
Group 1	(with teacher): Shane, Davontay, and Jessica Activity: Given photos depicting 17 steps to withdraw money from a bank machine, students will put photos in chronological order and verbally describe each step to the teacher. Materials: Three sets of 17 photos
Group 2	(with paraprofessional): Max, Lucia, and Juan Activity: Given role play using a teacher-made bank machine, students will complete steps to withdraw $20. Materials: Teacher-made bank machine, three 20-dollar bills
Group 3	(independent): Ginny and Melissa Activity: Computer-based instruction via laptop computer using video footage and still photographs (Mechling, 2004) Materials: CD-ROM and laptop for each student
Tuesday	**Skill area: Bank machine skills**
Group 1	(with paraprofessional): Max, Lucia, and Juan Activity: Given photos depicting 17 steps to withdraw money from a bank machine, students will put photos in chronological order and verbally describe each step to the teacher. Materials: Three sets of 17 photos
Group 2	(with teacher): Ginny and Melissa Activity: Given role play using a teacher-made bank machine, students will complete steps to withdraw $20. Materials: Teacher-made bank machine, two 20-dollar bills
Group 3	(independent): Shane, Davontay, and Jessica Activity: Computer-based instruction via laptop computer using video footage and still photographs (Mechling, 2004) Materials: CD-ROM and laptop for each student
Wednesday	**Skill area: Bank machine skills**
Group 1	(with paraprofessional): Ginny and Melissa Activity: Given photos depicting 17 steps to withdraw money from a bank machine, students will put photos in chronological order and verbally describe the steps to the teacher. Materials: Two sets of 17 photos
Group 2	(with teacher): Shane, Davontay, and Jessica Activity: Given role play using a teacher-made bank machine, students will complete steps to withdraw $20. Materials: Teacher-made bank machine, three 20-dollar bills
Group 3	(independent): Max, Lucia, and Juan Activity: Computer-based instruction via laptop computer using video footage and still photographs (Mechling, 2004) Materials: CD-ROM and laptop for each student
Thursday	**Skill area: Bank machine skills**
Follow plan for Monday	
Friday	**Skill area: Bank machine skills**
CBI Location: Best Bank on Willmore Avenue Materials: Notecard depicting personal identification number for each student Group 1 (with teacher): Ginny and Shane Group 2 (with paraprofessional): Jessica and Juan Group 3 (with occupational therapist): Melissa and Davontay Group 4 (with volunteer): Max	

Figure 3.4. Sample plan for a week of simulated instruction paired with community-based instruction to teach automated teller machine skills.

(CTD) guarantees errorless learning. Second, designing task analyses breaks complex tasks into discrete steps. Third, teaching students to self-monitor via audio prompting supports students' independence in a variety of settings. Finally, training for generalization facilitates learners' use of skills in the settings and situations where they actually need them.

Table 3.5. Examples of data collection when pairing community-based instruction with simulated instruction

Instructional content	Simulated instruction	Community-based instruction	Data collection
Providing personal information at a doctor's office and waiting to be seen	Role-playing, including telling name to secretary in school and being called to be seen	Visiting local doctor's office for an appointment	Daily (using a task analysis) in simulated setting as well as in doctor's office
Finding a seat at a basketball game	Using a map of the arena to identify where the seat is and role-playing with teacher appropriate manner to ask for assistance if needed at school	Attending a basketball game and finding seat with least-to-most prompting	Daily (using a task analysis) in simulated setting as well as at basketball game
Identifying aisle signs in the grocery store	Instruction via constant time delay for aisle sign words as well as additional practice in sorting items to be found in various aisles in the classroom	Going to grocery store to find items on a grocery list using aisle signs	Daily (using a task analysis) in simulated setting as well as in grocery store

Constant Time Delay

CTD is an instructional strategy that includes two phases. Initial instruction is the first phase of CTD, in which the teacher provides a target stimulus and a controlling stimulus simultaneously. In later trials (i.e., the second phase), the teacher provides the target stimulus and waits for a predetermined amount of time (i.e., the time delay). Finally, the teacher's next actions are based on student performance. In the event that the student does not respond or responds incorrectly, the teacher provides the controlling stimulus. If the student responds appropriately, the teacher may provide feedback (e.g., verbal praise, smile).

The zero-second delay trials provide an opportunity for errorless learning because students are provided with the question or direction, as well as the appropriate response, at the same time. For example, to teach a student to read the word *exit* using CTD, the teacher should point to the word in print and say, "What word?" (i.e., the target stimulus). Then the teacher should immediately say, "Exit" (i.e., the controlling stimulus). In later trials, a predetermined amount of time (3–5 seconds) should be inserted between the target stimulus and the controlling stimulus. For example, the teacher should point to the word in print and say, "What word?" (i.e., the target stimulus). Then the teacher would insert a wait time of about 4 seconds to allow for a student's unprompted response. If the student does not respond, the teacher would then say, "Exit" (i.e., the controlling stimulus). If a student provides the incorrect response, such as "enter," the teacher should immediately provide the controlling stimulus by saying "exit." In subsequent sessions, the teacher should implement zero-second delay trials again for this word. If a student provides the correct response, the teacher may choose to provide feedback in the form of verbal praise or other reward. When the student provides the correct response, the teacher would continue to implement the 4-second delay in subsequent sessions.

Given the errorless learning afforded to students via CTD, it is a valuable strategy in and out of the classroom. Additionally, research indicates that time delay is effective for teaching a variety of skills important to community participation. See Figure 3.5 for an example and Table 3.6 for a brief overview of research support for CTD.

The situation: Meisha cannot read the word *exit*. You, as the teacher, decide to implement constant time delay (CTD) instruction.	
Type of instruction: CTD in simulated and community-based settings	
Phase 1: Zero-second delay trial	
Guidelines: The teacher provides the target stimulus and the controlling stimulus at the same time. No delay or "wait time" is inserted in the first phase.	*Example:* The teacher points to the word in print and says, "What word? Exit." "What word?" is the target stimulus. "Exit" is the controlling stimulus.
Teacher actions	**Student action**
1. Point to word, "Exit," in print 2. Say: "What word? Exit"	1. Attend to teacher actions 2. Says, "Exit."
Phase 2: Four-second delay trial	
Guidelines: The teacher provides the target stimulus. A delay or "wait time" is inserted in the second phase. Based on student actions, the teacher will implement one of the following actions: • Given no student response, or an incorrect student response, provide the controlling stimulus • Given correct student response within the allocated time, acknowledge correct student response	*Example:* The teacher points to the word in print and says, "What word?" A 4-second delay is implemented. If student does not respond or responds incorrectly, the teacher says, "Exit." If the student responds correctly, the teacher might provide feedback by saying, "Good job!"
Teacher actions	**Student action**

1. Point to the word exit in print
2. Say: "What word?"
3. Wait a predetermined amount of time, in this case, 4 seconds
4. Respond as follows:
    a. For correct student response (i.e., "Exit"), teacher may provide praise.
    b. For incorrect student response (e.g., "Exert"), or no response, teacher will tell word (i.e., "Exit").
	1. Attend to teacher actions
	2. Respond in one of the following manners
	    a. Correctly
	    b. Incorrectly
	    c. No response

Figure 3.5.   Constant time delay.

TASK ANALYSIS WITH WHOLE TASK CHAINING

To identify the component parts of complex tasks, teachers use task analysis. To develop a task analysis, a teacher must conduct several steps. First, the teacher should identify a task to be completed. Second, the teacher should list the observable steps required for task completion. Finally, to be sure that all steps of the task are included in the appropriate order,

Table 3.6.   Research supporting the use of constant time delay (CTD)

Researchers	What was taught?	How?
Cuvo and Klatt (1992)	Sight words	Using CTD, researchers taught nine words in groups of three using flash cards in a school setting, video recordings in a school setting, and naturally occurring signs in the community.
Branham, Collins, Schuster, and Kleinert (1999)	Banking, street crossing, and mailing skills	Using CTD with one of the following techniques: classroom simulation plus community-based instruction (CBI), video modeling plus CBI, video modeling plus classroom simulation plus CBI
Morse and Schuster (2000)	Grocery shopping skills	Using CTD with simulation training using a storyboard to construct sequence of skills used when shopping for groceries

the teacher should field-test the task analysis. At this point, the task analysis is ready for use. To gain skills using a task analysis, students learn to perform individual steps in the chain and progress toward completing the entire task. By using the whole task chaining method, students complete all steps in the task analysis sequentially, every time they complete the sequence. The instructor provides assistance as necessary only for those steps with which the student requires assistance.

In the classroom, a teacher may use task analysis to teach students to use a calculator or hang up their coats in the closet. Further, task analysis can be used to teach skills for home, such as washing clothes and completing hygiene tasks, as well as tasks for the community, such as using a bus to get around and stocking shelves at work. A wealth of research indicates that task analysis instruction is effective in teaching community-referenced skills (see Table 3.7).

Task analysis is an essential tool for teaching complex skill sequences for the classroom, as well as a variety of other settings.

When teaching in the community, whole task chaining (Certo, Mezzullo, & Hunter, 1985) has several advantages. First, students practice every step of the task analysis each time the skill is taught. Second, the steps are taught and learned in the order in which they naturally occur. Third, by using whole task chaining, students are not required to repeatedly perform individual steps, which might be frustrating or boring; however, if a student does not demonstrate a particular step in the task analysis consistently, it may be helpful to practice that step in isolation. Fourth, practicing the whole task, rather than parts of the task, is most efficient in light of limits that may be placed on time allocated for CBI. At each round of training, the task is completed (e.g., an item is purchased, a load of laundry is clean, students arrive at a destination).

SELF-MANAGEMENT VIA AUDIO PROMPTING

Self-management via audio prompting is a strategy often used when teaching community-referenced skills. This strategy works by creating a task analysis (described in the previous section) for a specific skill using an audio device (e.g., tape recorder, digital audio recorder, MP3 player, computer) to record each step in the task chain. Using such a strategy has several benefits. First, it can be used in simulated and CBI settings. Additionally, it allows the student more flexibility in the pace of task completion and requires less teacher time. Finally, after successful completion of a step, it gives the student responsibility in moving forward to each subsequent step in the task chain.

Self-management with audio prompting is often accompanied by a least-to-most prompting hierarchy. When a student does not begin performing a task in the chain

Table 3.7.   Research supporting the use of task analysis

Researchers	What was taught?	How?
Vandercook (1991)	Leisure skills, including bowling and pinball	Using task analysis in a bowling alley
Haring, Breen, Weiner, Kennedy, and Bednersh (1995)	Purchasing skills	Using task analysis in bookstores, convenience stores, drugstores, gift shops, grocery stores, hobby shops, record stores
Taber, Alberto, Hughes, and Seltzer (2002)	Using a cell phone when lost	Using task analysis in a grocery store, public library, department store

correctly after the audio instruction has been played, the least-to-most prompt sequence can be initiated by the teacher. Self-evaluation strategies can also be included within the audio prompts. For example, if a step in a task analysis for washing clothes includes the directions of "put basket on floor in front of dryer," the audio may include, "Is the washer empty? Great! Now put the basket of clothes in front of the dryer." This example provides a self-evaluation of the previous step and reinforcement through verbal praise, all without the need of direct teacher support.

A plethora of research has been conducted to support the use of self-monitoring via audio prompting to teach community-referenced skills to students with mild and moderate disabilities. The acquisition of daily living skills, such as baking a microwave cake (Trask-Tyler, Grossi, & Heward, 1994) and using a washing machine (Briggs et al., 1990), has proven successful when using self-monitoring via audio prompting. See Table 3.8 for a brief overview of research that employed self-monitoring via audio prompting to teach daily living skills.

TRAINING FOR GENERALIZATION

Training for generalization involves teaching in a manner that supports students' use of skills in situations and settings different than the initial training settings and situations. To facilitate generalization of skills, researchers have identified a number of different strategies, including, but not limited to, the following (Stokes & Baer, 1977):

- Programming common stimuli
- Mediating generalization
- Teaching functional target behaviors
- Training loosely
- Using natural maintaining contingencies
- Training sufficient exemplars

When teachers plan community-referenced instruction, they should also make a plan for supporting generalization by selecting at least one of these strategies.

When teachers plan community-referenced instruction, they should also make a plan for supporting generalization so that students can perform the skills in different settings and situations, with different people, and using different materials.

Programming Common Stimuli

To program common stimuli, teachers attempt to replicate conditions from the generalization setting and embed them in initial instruction. In other words, during instruction,

Table 3.8. Research supporting the use of audio-prompting systems

Researchers	What was taught?	How?
Alberto, Taber, and Fredrick (1999)	Self-monitoring to decrease of off-task and aberrant behaviors in work settings and during transitional times between settings	Using self-operated audio-prompting system in community and work settings
Briggs et al. (1990)	Home-maintenance tasks	Using self-operated audio-prompting system in school (e.g., bathroom, home living suite) and community settings (e.g., laundromat)
Trask-Tyler et al. (1994)	Cooking skills	Using audio-recorded task analyses of recipes

teachers use materials or mimic conditions that are the same as those the student will use in generalized settings. For example, during classroom simulated instruction, teachers should use real money instead of fake bills during role-play activities in the classroom, as these materials are present in authentic purchasing situations. One challenge in implementing this strategy can be difficulty in creating materials.

Mediating Generalization

To mediate generalization, teachers provide instruction on a cobehavior. Instruction in this cobehavior is designed to assist the student in generalizing target skills to new settings and situations. Specifically, the cobehavior serves as an intermediary between performing the skill in the initial training setting and performing skills in generalized settings and situations. For example, during classroom instruction, a teacher may require students to write a list of homework assignments and check off assignments as they are completed. This listing strategy can then mediate students' generalization of additional skills such as grocery shopping (i.e., using a grocery list) and job completion (i.e., using a to-do list).

Teaching Functional Target Behaviors

When students are taught skills that are needed and used on a day-to-day basis (possibly community referenced), they are more likely to be reinforced in the natural environment, which in turn will support skill generalization. Conversely, when students are taught skills that are not essential for everyday life, these skills are not likely to occur in new situations and settings. For example, during classroom instruction, a teacher may teach students to use language for a purpose (e.g., requesting a drink) rather than when directed (e.g., "Say *milk, please*").

Training Loosely

By training loosely, teachers allow naturally occurring situations to prompt and reinforce students' performance, as opposed to intervening to provide precise prompts and specific types of reinforcement. To train loosely, teachers do not strictly control the instructional conditions, as the conditions under which students will perform skills vary across settings and situations. For example, on twice-weekly trips to different grocery stores, students should use a variety of clerks and checkout aisles at the store. The teacher should not intervene to provide precise prompting and reinforcement. Rather, the teacher should allow the situation to naturally prompt and reinforce, as these conditions will best prepare students to perform the skill.

Using Natural Maintaining Contingencies

To employ natural maintaining contingencies, teachers should select skills for instruction that will later be reinforced naturally in the environment in which the behavior typically occurs. Conversely, skills that will typically be reinforced via artificial means (e.g., candy, sticker) will pose challenges in terms of facilitating generalization, as these reinforcers are not routinely available in community settings. For example, purchasing skills should be taught in the school cafeteria. Natural maintaining contingencies are the food items that are purchased and consumed.

Training Sufficient Exemplars

Using sufficient exemplars in training involves teaching students in a manner that prepares them to perform a target skill in the wide array of situations where it is needed. To represent the various situations in which students must perform the skill, teachers should evaluate the numerous settings and situations in which students will be expected to perform the skill and systematically represent these characteristics in instruction. For example, when teaching banking skills, students should use many different ATMs rather than one particular location.

Given that these strategies are research based, students are more likely to generalize the skills to new environments—that is, to perform skills in the variety of settings in which the skills are needed. See Table 3.9 for examples of how each generalization strategy can be used to support community-referenced instruction.

SUMMARY

Special educators face the unique challenge of balancing instruction involving academic content standards with the essential skills necessary to improve the postsecondary engagement and independence of students with disabilities. Although most typically developing students acquire these functional skills through exposure in natural settings, many students with disabilities need explicit instruction to learn, maintain, and generalize these skills. The challenge of providing this type of instruction comes with no easy solutions, but the effective

Table 3.9. Generalization of skills

Strategy	Example
Program common stimuli	During instruction related to ordering food at a fast-food restaurant, a teacher may embed (or program) terminology typically employed by a cashier at a fast-food restaurant (e.g., "May I take your order?"), so that this cue (or stimulus) is consistent between where the skill is taught and where the skills will eventually be needed.
Mediate generalization	Teach students to organize materials from left-to-right to teach a variety of topics, including dealing cards to play blackjack. At work, students will be taught to organize materials (e.g., cloth napkin, knives, forks, spoons) needed to wrap silverware using the same left-to-right behavior.
Teach functional target behaviors	Teach students to use money to purchase items in the school cafeteria, as this skill will be functional in a variety of settings and situations.
Train loosely	Teach interviewing skills for employment. Set up mock interviews with people unfamiliar to the student. Do not provide the interviewer with questions for the students, as students will likely face a variety of questions and interview styles when applying for positions.
Use natural maintaining contingencies	Teach students to maintain personal hygiene and cleanliness. Natural maintaining contingencies are the compliments and looks of approval the student will receive from peers and others.
Train sufficient exemplars	Teach cell phone skills. Use a variety of cell phones in instruction so that students are prepared to use a variety of cell phones, rather than one particular brand or model.

teaching strategies described in this chapter make such a juggling act more manageable. Perhaps even more important, the strategies discussed in this chapter improve the likelihood that students will not only acquire these essential skills, but will use these skills to increase their independence and quality of life long after exit from school.

FOR FURTHER INFORMATION

Life-Centered Career Education (LCCE) Curriculum (http://www.cec.sped.org)

The LCCE is a transition-focused curriculum that is endorsed by the Council for Exceptional Children. The main components include instructional recommendations for teaching daily living skills, personal social skills, and occupational skills.

Tool Kit on Teaching and Assessing Students with Disabilities (http://www.osepideasthatwork .org/toolkit)

The tool kit is a product developed by the U.S. Department of Education, Office of Special Education Programs. This resource includes current research briefs and materials to support special educators in selecting appropriate strategies for teaching and assessing students with disabilities.

4

Data Collection Strategies

Valerie L. Mazzotti and David W. Test

With the current educational focus on student and teacher accountability, it is important for teachers to be able to clearly document the effects of their instruction on student learning. As a result, it is important for teachers to collect meaningful data to show students are learning new skills. Data collection is also included as part of the Taxonomy for Transition Programming (Kohler, 1996)–specifically, in the area of student development. Within this area, data collection can be used to assess student skill acquisition related to academic skills, life skills, and employment skills. Alberto and Troutman (2009) suggested three reasons why teachers should collect data:

1. Collecting data allows teachers to accurately determine the effects of an intervention or instruction. Did the intervention work or not?

2. Ongoing data collection allows both summative and formative data-based decision making. By collecting data as the intervention is happening, teachers are able to adjust their teaching to meet student needs.

3. Collecting and reporting data is the ultimate tool of accountability.

At the same time, given the increasing responsibilities of teachers, it is also important to provide teachers with data collection strategies that are both effective and efficient. This chapter will describe a process to do that. First, we describe the different types (or dimensions) of behavior about which data can be collected. Once teachers decide on a type of behavior, this will lead them to the data collection strategy. Finally, teachers must decide who will collect the data, how often it will need to be collected, and how to display the data.

DIMENSIONS OF BEHAVIOR

In determining effective instructional practices for secondary students with disabilities, teachers should use ongoing evaluation and data collection to determine if specific instructional strategies being implemented are working. The process of collecting data on students' acquisition of transition-related skills should begin with the classroom teacher identifying the new skills to be taught, determining specific skill deficits (i.e., target behaviors) exhibited by students, and identifying a measurement system to evaluate the desired behavior change.

Choosing a specific data collection system will allow for assessment of specific transition-related skills to provide teachers with information for planning and developing effective instruction for secondary students with disabilities (Alberto & Troutman, 2009; Cooper, Heron, & Heward, 2007). As such, these data collection systems become part of the ongoing, informal transition assessment process described in Chapter 2.

The first step in developing a data collection system is to identify the dimensions of the behavior to be taught. Dimensions can be divided into two types: *count it* and *time it*. Deciding which dimension of a behavior to collect data on is the first step in the data collection process and requires determining whether the target behavior should be counted or timed.

Count It

When determining if a behavior falls into the count it category, teachers should consider whether the target behavior can be counted individually based on the number of occurrences (e.g., number of steps in the task analysis completed, number of times out of seat, number of callouts during class). When the number of behaviors is counted, this is called the *frequency count*.

Frequency

Frequency counts involve simply counting the number of times a student engages in a target behavior (Alberto & Troutman, 2009; Cooper et al., 2007). The following are examples of reporting data on the frequency of a secondary student's transition related skill development (target behavior):

- Count the number of grocery sight words read during community-based instruction.
- Count the number of steps completed correctly on the task analysis to withdraw money from an automated teller machine (ATM).
- Count the number of items completed correctly on a job application.
- Count the number of times a student inappropriately touches others when meeting employers during community-based instruction.

To determine the frequency of the target behavior, the teacher must count the number of times the target behavior occurs within a specified observational period. By always counting the number of behaviors during the same length of time, educators can compare the numbers from day to day. If the length of time changes, then numbers cannot be compared.

Rate

The rate must be used if the observation periods vary in length. Rate refers to frequency expressed in relation to time. For example, to compare the number of behaviors that occur in 30 minutes to the number that occur in 60 minutes, data must be converted to rate. When considering rate as the measurement system, teachers should count the number of times a student engages in a target behavior and then divide by the length of time the behavior was observed (Alberto & Troutman, 2009; Cooper et al., 2007). Some examples of using rate to measure specific transition-related skills include the following:

- The number of recreational sight words read correctly were eight in 2 minutes on Day 1 (rate = 4 per minute) and eight in 4 minutes on Day 2 (rate = 2 per minute).
- A student was out of her seat five times during a 45-minute functional math lesson on Day 1 (rate = 0.11 per minute) and two times during a 30-minute reading lesson (rate = 0.07 per minute).

Time It

If it is important for the target behavior to occur over time (e.g., how long did it take to complete an assignment, how long did the student stay on task) or if it is important to initiate the target behavior in a timely manner (e.g., time it takes to begin a job task, time it takes to get materials), teachers should use time it as a method for measuring the target behavior. The length of time a behavior occurs is called *duration* and the length of time it takes to start a behavior is called *latency*.

Duration

Duration refers to the amount of time that a student engages in a target behavior. It is typically measured using standard units of time (i.e., minutes, seconds, or hours). Duration should be considered when examining how long a student engages in a target behavior versus the number of times (i.e., frequency) a student engages in the target behavior (Alberto & Troutman, 2009; Cooper et al., 2007). The following are examples of using duration to measure specific transition-related skills:

- Time how long a student stays focused on the job-related task.
- Time how long it takes a student to complete the job application.
- Time how long a student works on the self-advocacy project.

Latency

Latency refers to the length of time between providing a student with an instruction to perform a target behavior and when the student actually starts the target behavior. Latency should be considered when a teacher wants to determine how long it takes for a student to initiate the target behavior after a request has been made (Alberto & Troutman, 2009; Cooper et al., 2007). The following are examples of using latency to measure specific transition-related skills:

- Time how long it takes a student to begin a work task after the job coach asked her to start.
- Time how long it takes a student to begin reading a list of functional reading sight words after the teacher asked her to begin reading.
- Time how long it takes for a student to begin entering data after his employer asked him to start.

DATA COLLECTION STRATEGIES

Once the specific dimension of behavior has been determined, the next step is to determine the best method for collecting data on the target behavior. When using count it, event recording is the primary method used for collecting data on specific target behaviors. When using time it, momentary time sampling, duration recording, or latency recording are the methods used. See Table 4.1 for dimensions of behavior and data collection systems.

Event Recording

The recording system that should be used when collecting data using count it is called *event recording*. Event recording involves recording the number of times a target behavior occurs within a prespecified time period (Alberto & Troutman, 2009; Cooper et al., 2007). Event recording can be calculated as a number, rate, and/or percent, which makes it an easy and efficient method for teachers to use.

Methods for collecting event recording data can be simple and effective for classroom teachers. There are several methods for collecting data using an event recording system, including simple tally marks, task analyses, and counting devices.

Tally Marks

When counting the number of times a target behavior occurs within a specified amount of time, a teacher may use a simple tally mark system. A tally mark system may include using slash marks, numbers, or other methods (e.g., paper clips, pennies) to collect data on the number of times a target behavior occurs. For example, the teacher may use tally marks to determine how many times a student was out of his or her seat during instruction. Tally marks may also be used to determine the rate of the behavior. For example, the teacher may use tally marks to determine how many times a student was out of his or her seat during the first 15 minutes of instruction and then calculate the number of times out of seat per minute.

Table 4.1. Dimensions of behavior and data collection systems

Dimensions of behavior	Data collection systems
Count it	**Event recording**
Use frequency counts when interested in the number of behaviors that occur within a set period of time.	Count the number of times a behavior occurs within a period of time
Use rate counts when the observation time period varies from day to day.	
Time it	**Duration recording**
Use when interested in the amount of time a behavior occurs or if interested in amount of time between when a request is made and when the task is started	Use a stopwatch to collect the total amount of time a behavior occurred.
	Momentary time sampling
	Record if a behavior is occurring by looking at the end of a predetermined interval.
	Latency recording
	Record the amount of time between a prompt and when a behavior begins.

Task Analysis

Another way to collect data using event recording is to use a task analysis (see Chapter 3). A task analysis provides a list of essential steps required to complete a specific task, as well as a step-by-step format that breaks a complex skill into smaller, teachable units.

When using task analysis, the teacher simply counts the number of steps a student completes correctly. If the total number of steps in the task analysis is always the same, then the teacher should record the number correct. If the total number of steps changes, then the teacher should divide the number of steps correct by the total number of steps possible and calculate the percent correct.

Finally, the National Secondary Transition Technical Assistance Center (NSTTAC, 2009) has identified total task chaining as an evidence-based practice to teach a variety of functional skills to secondary students with disabilities. Specifically, the practices include using total task chaining to teach functional life skills (i.e., purchasing, home maintenance, and leisure skills).

Task analysis is one method that researchers have used to collect data on student acquisition of secondary transition-related skills. For example, Mechling, Gast, and Langone (2002) used a task analysis to collect data on the number of correct student responses for locating 12 grocery items on a grocery list and identifying the corresponding grocery aisle signs both in simulated and real-life grocery store settings.

Counting Devices

Various types of counting devices (e.g., wrist counters, digital counters) can help teachers collect data on the frequency or rate of a target behavior (Alberto & Troutman, 2009). Wrist counters can be used to collect data on the frequency of the student's target behavior and allow the teacher to count each occurrence of the target behavior with discretion. When using wrist counters to collect data, teachers have a method for tallying the target behavior, which allows for up to 99 responses. Based on the number of times the target behavior occurs, the wrist counter can be used to count the frequency of the target behavior.

Handheld digital tally counters are similar to wrist counters in that they also allow for step-by-step recording of the behavior occurrence. Handheld digital counters are another effective and efficient device that can be used to collect frequency or rate data on specific target behaviors. For example, these digital counters can be used to tally a student's target behavior during community-based instruction.

There are also simple, economical methods for collecting event recording data that may be more cost-effective and efficient for the classroom teacher. These methods include the teacher making marks on masking tape stuck to his or her clothing to record the number of times a behavior occurs, moving paper clips from one pocket to the other each time the behavior occurs, or simply using a small calculator in a discrete location such as a pocket or desk (Alberto & Troutman, 2009; Cooper et al., 2007). See Table 4.2 for more examples of data collection.

Momentary Time Sampling

Momentary time sampling may be the most time-efficient method for teachers to use when collecting data using the time it strategy. With momentary time sampling, an observation

Table 4.2. Examples of target behaviors, dimensions, and recording systems

Target behavior	Dimension	Recording system and how it is used
Reading recreational sight words orally	Count it	Event recording: Using tally marks, count number of recreational recreational sight words read correctly
Doing laundry during community-based instruction	Count it	Event recording: Using a task analysis, count number of steps completed on a task analysis for doing laundry
Exhibiting disruptive classroom behavior (e.g., out of seat during instruction, calling out, chair rocking)	Count it	Event recording: Using a counting device, move paper clips from one pocket to the other to count number of times student exhibits disruptive behavior during community job task
Talking to a peer when student should be working independently on a job task	Time it	Momentary time sampling: Set a timer to ring every 3 minutes; at end of each interval, observe student and record occurrence of target behavior
Cleaning a bathroom during community-based instruction	Time it	Duration recording: Record length of time it takes student to complete cleaning bathroom
Completing a job application	Time it	Latency recording: Record length of time for student to begin completing job application after teacher asks

period is split into equal intervals (no longer than 3 minutes). The teacher then records whether or not the target behavior occurred at the end of each timed interval. When using momentary time sampling, the teacher can set a timer to ring at the end of a specific interval (e.g., 1 minute, 2 minutes, 3 minutes), at which time the teacher observes and records the occurrence of the target behavior.

Duration and Latency Recording

When collecting data on the duration or latency of a target behavior, consideration should be made with regard to the length of time a specific target behavior lasts and/or the length of time it takes for a student to initiate the target behavior. Duration and latency are measured using standard units of time (i.e., minutes or seconds). When deciding on which method to use for collecting duration or latency data, two questions should be considered:

1. Are you concerned with how long the target behavior lasts? If so, use duration recording.

2. Are you concerned with how long it takes for the target behavior to begin? If so, use latency recording.

Duration Recording

When teachers are concerned about how long a target behavior lasts, they can use a duration recording system. Duration is measured using standard units of time. For example, if the teacher is concerned with how long a student stays engaged in a work-related task (e.g., cleaning bathrooms, collating and photocopying, sorting office supplies), a duration recording system would allow the teacher to record the length of time the student is actually engaged in the work-related behavior based on the number of minutes or seconds the student is engaged.

When using duration recording, the teacher should determine a specific length of time during which the target behavior would be recorded (e.g., 10-minute time frame). In the example of the student engaging in the work-related task, during a 10-minute time frame the teacher should record the length of time the student engages in the work-related task. The student may engage in the work-related task for the first 2 minutes of the 10-minute time frame and then may only engage in the work-related task for 1.5 minutes at the end of the 10-minute time frame. This would result in a total duration of 3.5 minutes engaged in the work-related task.

Latency Recording

When teachers are concerned with how long it takes for the target behavior to begin, they may use a latency recording system. Similar to duration, latency is measured using standard units of time (i.e., minutes or seconds). In the example of a student's engagement in a work-related task, a job coach may ask the student to begin the task during community-based instruction. The teacher would then time how long it takes for the student to actually begin the work-related task after instructions were provided by the job coach. To record latency data, the teacher would begin recording the time at which the student was given a cue to begin a specific response and the actual time it took for the student to respond to the instructions. See Table 4.2 for more examples of data collection using the time it method.

Latency recording can be used to collect data on a variety of behaviors. Shevin and Klein (2004) suggested that teachers use latency recording as one method to collect data about student on-task behavior while participating in tasks in which choices were made.

DATA COLLECTION ISSUES

Teachers need to try to choose data collection strategies that are fairly unobtrusive and still provide sufficient data to determine training effectiveness. As teachers plan for data collection, they should consider the following questions:

1. Who should collect data?
2. How often should data be collected?
3. How should data be displayed?

Who Should Collect the Data?

Data can be collected by either the teacher or the student. Having the student record his or her own performance (sometimes called self-monitoring or self-recording) may itself increase the likelihood of independent performance. In addition, self-monitoring is unobtrusive because the student can record his or her own data and then review it with the teacher at a later time.

How Often Should the Data Be Collected?

In the past, teachers often stood over their students with clipboards in hand, recording every behavior. This data collection strategy was justified by the need to collect data on each step taught in a school or workplace. However, not every response needs to be recorded; teachers now have realized the effectiveness of conducting probes to obtain information about learner performance. Using probes, the teacher can teach for a while and then step back, watch the student perform the task without providing assistance, and collect data. Probes help teachers avoid the difficult problem of trying to teach and collect data at the same time. The idea is to collect only enough data to allow instructional decisions to be made—that is, to determine if the student is learning the skill.

For example, a teacher might teach a new skill by prompting a student through a task analysis three times and then conducting a data collection probe. To do this, the teacher should ask the student to try performing the task without assistance while the teacher collects data using the task analysis. The teacher should start by collecting at least one probe each day the skill is taught. Once a skill is mastered (e.g., performed correctly three times in a row), the teacher should switch to a once-a-week probe. After three weekly probes, the teacher can switch to monthly probes.

How Should the Data Be Displayed?

If every picture tells a story, then the best way to display data may be to graph it. Figure 4.1 is a typical graph showing the number of steps completed correctly on a 10-step task analysis for using an ATM. As can be seen by looking at the graph, LaShawndra's performance using the ATM is improving each day. However, although the number of correct steps is improving, the graph does not show which steps LaShawndra is performing correctly. To know this, the teacher would have to look at the data collection sheet and the graph together.

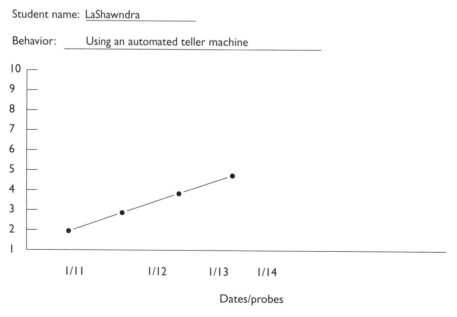

Figure 4.1. Typical graph showing student performance on a 10-step task analysis for using an automated teller machine.

Figure 4.2 shows a solution to this problem. By using a self-graphing format, both correct and incorrect steps can be viewed, as well as the total steps correct. To create a self-graphing task analysis data collection form, follow these steps:

1. Write the steps of the task analysis in reverse order, with the last step at the top of the form.

2. As the student performs each step, mark correct steps with an *X*.

3. Once the student has completed the entire task, count the number of *X*s and circle that number on the form

4. Connect the circles to create data points as on a normal graph.

In this way, the teacher can know what steps a student is performing correctly, as well as have a graph of student progress from day to day—all on the same form.

SUMMARY

Data collection should make the teacher's job easier. By knowing how students are performing on the skills they are teaching, teachers can modify their instruction as needed to be as effective and efficient as possible. Think of students' data as their vital signs. If doctors did not collect data on their patients' vital signs, they would not be able to tell if their patients were in good or bad health. In the same way for teachers, students' performance data are vital signs. Performance data allow teachers to be effective, efficient, and accountable for the instruction in the classroom.

Student name: LaShawndra

Behavior: Using an automated teller machine

10	Remove receipt	10	10	10	10	10	10
9	Remove card	9	X	X	X	9	9
8	Press *end transaction* button	8	8	X	X	8	8
7	Lift door and remove bills	7	7	7	7	7	7
6	Press *correct* button	6	6	6	6	6	6
5	Enter dollar amount	5	5	5	(5)	5	5
4	Press *withdraw from checking* button	4	4	(4)	4	4	4
3	Press button indicating PIN is correct	3	(3)	3	X	3	3
2	Enter PIN	(X)	X	X	X	2	2
1	Insert card	1	1	1	1	1	1
	Dates	1/11	1/12	1/13	1/14		

Figure 4.2.   Self-graphing task analysis of 10-step task analysis for using an automated teller machine. (*Key:* X, correct step; O, total number correct.)

FOR FURTHER INFORMATION

Data Collection Resources

Doing What Works (http://dww.ed.gov/)

Doing What Works is sponsored by the U.S. Department of Education and translates research-based practices identified by the Institute for Education Sciences into practical tools teachers can use in the classroom. The web site provides information about how to monitor student progress and collect data related to the implementation of evidence-based and research-based practices.

The Center on Positive Behavioral Interventions and Supports (http://www.pbis.org/default.aspx)

The Center on Positive Behavioral Interventions and Supports is a technical assistance center funded by the Office of Special Education Programs. The center provides capacity-building information and technical assistance for identifying, adapting, and sustaining effective schoolwide disciplinary practices. The center provides a variety of resources and information for teachers and schools related to processes for collecting data on student behavior.

The National Secondary Transition Technical Assistance Center (http://www.nsttac.org/ LessonPlanLibrary/StudentFocusedPlanning.aspx)

The NSTTAC is funded by the U.S. Department of Education's Office of Special Education Programs and provides information related to evidence-based secondary transition practices for students with disabilities. The web site includes research-to-practice lesson plan starters that teachers can use to teach life skills, employment skills, self-determination skills, and academic skills to secondary students with disabilities. The lesson plans include objectives, settings and materials, content taught, teaching procedures, and methods for evaluation in order to collect data on student skill acquisition.

5

Student-Focused Planning

Nicole Uphold and Melissa Hudson

For many students, their years of school attendance culminate in the knowledge and skills needed to successfully transition from high school to adult life, including living on their own, getting and keeping a job, and/or continuing education in a postsecondary setting such as a community college, university, or technical school. Students with disabilities, however, may have a different experience (Blackorby & Wagner, 1996).

Data from the National Longitudinal Transition Study 2 documented the experiences of a national sample of students who were age 13–16 years in 2000 as they moved from secondary school into adult roles. Far fewer youth with disabilities were enrolled in postsecondary education and employed at 2 years post-school than youth without disabilities. Specifically, 19% of youth with disabilities were enrolled in postsecondary education compared with 40% of youth without disabilities. In addition, 41% of youth with disabilities were employed compared with 63% of their peers without disabilities (Wagner et al., 2005). Additionally, 28% of students with disabilities did not graduate with a diploma because they dropped out of high school (National Center for Special Education Research, 2005). The noncompletion rates for students with specific learning disabilities and emotional/behavior disorders were even higher, at 35% and 61%, respectively (U.S. Department of Education, 2003).

The future for students with disabilities who do not complete high school is bleak. Without a high school diploma, youth are more likely to experience lower wages, higher rates of imprisonment, and poorer health than peers who graduate (Cataldi, Laird, & KewalRamani, 2009). Student-focused planning is one strategy educators can use to keep students with disabilities in high school (Benz, Lindstrom, & Yovanoff, 2000). This chapter describes student-focused planning, its importance, and strategies educators can use to promote student-focused planning with their students.

STUDENT-FOCUSED PLANNING

Student-focused planning is one of the five categories of effective transition practices in the Taxonomy for Transition Programming (Kohler, 1996). Student-focused planning includes the development of a student's individualized education program (IEP) and strategies for promoting student participation in their transition planning. In student-focused planning, educational decisions are based on the student's goals and interests. After setting relevant goals, students plan, make decisions, and evaluate progress toward attaining their goals (Martin, Marshall, & Maxson, 1993; Ward & Kohler, 1996). Questions for students to consider during transition planning are included in Table 5.1.

RATIONALE FOR INVOLVING STUDENTS IN TRANSITION PLANNING

From preparing students for high-stakes testing to completing the paperwork required by special education due process and individualized instruction, educators have many demands on their time. Finding time to involve students in their transition planning may seem difficult and unnecessary. However, by involving students in their transition process, educators not only accomplish the immediate task at hand (i.e., meaningful transition planning for students), but they may also encourage behaviors that will benefit the student for many years to come. Table 5.2 describes six reasons found in the literature for involving students with disabilities in their transition planning.

First, involving students in transition planning provides students with opportunities to make important decisions about their lives. As noted in Chapter 2, the student's individual choices, preferences, and needs in the areas of education and training, employment, adult living arrangements, and community experiences are the heart of student-focused planning. By increasingly taking responsibility in the planning process, students have opportunities to practice making important decisions for themselves.

Second, involving students in transition planning can enhance school completion. When students are involved in student-focused transition planning, research indicates that they are more likely to complete high school (Test, Fowler, White, Richter, & Walker, 2009b). For example, Repetto, Pankaskie, Hankins, and Schwartz (1997) conducted a survey that included students with mild disabilities and found student participation in the development of their IEP to be an effective practice for dropout prevention. Benz et al. (2000) examined the outcomes of school completion and employment for students with disabilities and components of a youth transition program. They found a positive correlation between student-focused planning strategies and high school completion. In addition, Izzo, Yurick, Nagaraja, and Novak (2010) found that integrating academic and career skills nurtured and enhanced students' ability to understand and retain content because it was relevant and meaningful to their lives. When students find their coursework to be relevant to their lives, they are more likely to continue in school.

Third, involving students in transition planning can promote postsecondary attendance and success. Nearly half of high school students with disabilities (i.e., 47%) reported that their primary transition goal was to attend college, but only 19% were actually enrolled in postsecondary education at 2 years post-school (Cameto, Levine, & Wager, 2004)—a

Table 5.1.   Questions for students to consider during transition planning

What are my school, work, and community living interests and skills?

Where do I want to go to school, live, or work after leaving high school?

What courses should I take to prepare for the future?

What are my strengths and what do I need to improve?

What do I need to learn to make my post-school goals happen?

From Martin, J.E., Van Dycke, J., D'Ottavio, M., & Nickerson, K. (2007). The student-directed summary of performance: Increasing student and family involvement in the transition planning process. *Career Development for Exceptional Children, 30*, 14; reprinted by permission.

Table 5.2.   Reasons to involve students with disabilities in their transition planning

To provide students with opportunities to make important decisions about their lives

To enhance school completion

To promote attendance and success in postsecondary settings

To encourage family involvement

To teach students lifelong skills, such as goal setting and attainment

To encourage independence (i.e., autonomy)

much lower percentage than youth without disabilities (i.e., 40%). Involvement in transition planning and IEP development may help students attain the goals they planned related to postsecondary school attendance and success.

Fourth, family involvement in student transition can promote positive post-school outcomes. In a qualitative study of the role of family in career development and post-school employment outcomes for young adults with learning disabilities, Lindstrom, Doren, Metheny, Johnson, and Zane (2007) found families who advocated for their child while they were in high school had higher wage jobs after graduation. Morningstar et al. (2010) found family involvement and support during transition to be correlated with student self-determination in postsecondary settings. Questions to help parents prepare for and participate in IEP meetings focused on transition planning are described in Table 5.3.

Next, students learn lifelong skills such as goal setting and attainment throughout the planning process. Students should be involved in the transition planning process so that their voices are heard and they have positive post-school outcomes. Students also should learn skills that they can take with them after graduation and use throughout their future life. For example, understanding their disabilities and the supports they need to be successful will allow students to advocate for themselves in higher education and on the job. Also, learning to set educational goals and work toward achieving them can generalize to setting goals throughout life.

Finally, transition planning provides opportunities for students to develop independence. The ultimate goal of special education is student independence (Shevin & Klein, 1984). In student-focused planning, many of the roles typically completed by adults gradually shift to students, which gives students an opportunity to be more independent. However, skills that enable students to be more independent may need to be taught. Martin et al. (2006) found that students led more IEP meetings and engaged in more IEP meeting leadership steps (e.g., introducing self, introducing team members, stating purpose of meeting) after specific instruction on IEP participation. Izzo et al. (2010) found that students who

Table 5.3.   Questions to help parents prepare for and participate in an IEP meeting focused on transition planning

What does your child want to do with his or her life?

What are your child's needs, abilities, and skills?

What programs, services, accommodations, or modifications are needed?

What kinds of accommodations will be needed in higher education or employment?

How can both practical and academic goals be included in the educational and transition programs?

What community-based training opportunities are provided by the school?

Are work experience classes appropriate to reach employment goals?

How could the educational and transition programs be more integrated into the regular program?

Key: IEP, individualized education program.

received web-based instruction on information technology (IT) within the context of transition planning activities not only made gains in IT skills, but also gained skills in goal setting, knowledge of how to find jobs, and information about college. In addition, Woods, Sylvester, and Martin (2010) found that students' perception of their ability to tell their IEP team about their education goals after high school graduation increased after instruction in student-directed transition planning.

STEPS FOR INVOLVING STUDENTS IN THE TRANSITION PLANNING PROCESS

The transition planning process is often viewed as a single IEP meeting that is held to develop postsecondary outcomes, decide activities and services that will help the student achieve desired outcomes, and write goals and objectives. However, the planning process is more than one meeting; it is a year-round process that focuses on longitudinal planning with the student.

Before students can be involved in their planning process, they may need to be taught related skills (see Table 5.4). Students will need to know how to ask questions and listen to others, as well as how to make decisions and solve problems. Students will also need basic self-awareness, including strengths, areas of need, likes, and dislikes.

In addition, the other participants in the planning process (e.g., teachers, parents, other education personnel, adult service providers) should have clear responsibilities related to their roles in the student-focused planning process. The special education teacher will need to provide information about student-focused planning and how each participant can assist with this. See Table 5.5 for suggestions on how a special education teacher can assist the other participants with student-focused planning.

The transition planning process consists of planning, drafting the IEP, meeting to revise the IEP, and implementing the IEP (Konrad & Test, 2004). Each of these areas will be discussed in more detail in the following sections.

Planning

The planning stage includes determining strengths and needs, establishing a long-term vision, organizing materials for the IEP meeting, and teaching students about the transition

Table 5.4.   Prerequisite skills and strategies for teaching

Skill	Teaching strategy
Asking questions	Role-play questions that students typically ask during individualized education program meetings.
Asking for help	Provide students with scenarios of when they would need to ask for help and have the students develop questions.
Listening	Have students practice following directions (e.g., give three-step directions and ask students to perform actions).
	Have students practice repeating what was said to them (e.g., telephone operator game).
Decision making	Provide students with sample decisions and work through the process together.
Problem solving	Provide students with problem scenarios and work through the process together.
Self-awareness	Have students complete inventories on perceived strengths, weaknesses, likes, and dislikes.
	Have students interview others to determine if their own view matches others' views.

Table 5.5. How to facilitate participants' roles in the planning process

Person	How to facilitate person's role
Parent	Provide information about the transition planning process.
	Ask about the parent's vision for the student's future.
	Provide a peer mentor (i.e., a parent of a child who has been through the transition process).
Regular education teacher	Provide information about the transition planning process.
	Request that the teacher meet with students (rather than the special education teacher) to discuss concerns.
Administrator	Request that the administrator avoid educational jargon.
	Have the administrator encourage all teachers to use student-focused planning.
Adult service provider	Provide information about the provider's agency to the student, not the parent.
	Request that all questions be addressed to the student first.
	Allow students to interview/visit to learn more about services.

process. Using commercially available curricula and person-centered planning methods, students have been able to state their strengths and needs, develop a long-term vision for their futures, and increase their transition awareness (Cross, Cooke, Wood, & Test, 1999; Keyes & Owens-Johnson, 2003; Powers, Turner, Matuszewski, Wilson, & Phillips, 2001). For example, the IEP template by Konrad and Test (2004) can be used to help students list their strengths and needs and develop their visions for after school (see Figure 5.1).

Konrad and Test (2004) taught middle school students to write drafts of their own IEPs using their IEP template. In addition to completing the template, students also increased their knowledge of IEPs.

Although the commercially available curricula tend to focus on working with students with high-incidence disabilities, person-centered planning methods have been used with students with significant disabilities. Using these planning methods, a support team is identified for each student and the team assists the student with developing a long-term vision and the necessary supports needed to help the student reach that vision. The key to this planning method is to invite a range of individuals who know both the student and the support that is available in the community. These people can provide an in-depth view of an individual and his or her strengths, needs, hopes, and dreams. One such person-centered planning method is the McGill Action Planning System (Forest & Lusthaus, 1990; see Figure 5.2), in which a facilitator asks each questions and each participant in the process has the opportunity to respond.

The foundation of person-centered planning is backward planning. In backward planning, a team of people assists the student with developing a long-term vision. From this vision, the team plans backward to create a long-term plan that assists the student with reaching this vision.

Drafting

The second phase of the process is drafting the IEP, during which the student chooses and writes goals, objectives, present level of performance, post-school goals, and services needed to achieve these goals. This preliminary work happens before the IEP meeting. It is important to remember that the IEP document will be formally completed at the IEP meeting

Vision Statement

Where do you see yourself in the future? What is the vision or dream you have for yourself? Make sure your vision reflects the high, yet realistic, expectations you hold for yourself. Also include expectations others may hold for you and results of research.

According to my career research, I would be good at . . .

_____

I agree / disagree (circle one) because . . .

_____

_____

My _____ (parent/guardian) hopes . . .

_____

_____

My _____ teacher thinks . . .

_____

_____

After high school, I plan to . . .

Live_____

Learn _____

Work _____

Play _____

In order to achieve this vision, the best high school course of study for me is _____

_____

Figure 5.1. Sample individualized education program template.

From Konrad, M., & Test, D.W. (2004). Teaching middle-school students with disabilities to use an IEP template. *Career Development for Exceptional Individuals, 27,* 101–124; reprinted by permission.

In *Evidence-Based Instructional Strategies for Transition* by David W. Test.
(2012, Paul H. Brookes Publishing Co., Inc.)

1. What is the individual's history?
2. What is your dream for the individual?
3. What is your nightmare?
4. Who is the individual?
5. What are the individual's strengths, gifts, and abilities?
6. What are the individual's needs?
7. What would the individual's ideal day at school look like and what must be done to make it happen?

Figure 5.2. Guiding questions from the McGill Action Planning System. (*Source:* Forest & Lusthaus, 1990.)

by the entire team. Teachers typically ask students about their goals and then use that information to formally write the goals for the IEP document. However, researchers have taught students how to develop IEP goals and objectives. Konrad and Test (2004) had students use an IEP template (see Figure 5.3) to write present levels of performance, goals, objectives, services, and accommodations. They also developed a self-regulated writing strategy in which students are taught to write an IEP goal, four objectives, and a timeline (Konrad & Test, 2007). The students then put this information into a paragraph for the IEP document (see Figure 5.4).

Meeting to Revise the Plan

In the third stage of the IEP process, students are involved in the IEP meeting. Educators should be aware that student attendance at the IEP meeting does not ensure students are actively involved in the meeting or that their interests, strengths, and preferences are considered by team members. On the contrary, research has found that the student may be the least involved team member (Martin, Huber Marshall, & Sale, 2004) who talks less than other team members (Martin et al., 2006) during the IEP meeting.

Fortunately, instruction on planning and attending IEP meetings has increased students' involvement in their IEP meetings. For example, Martin et al. (2006) found that students who received specific IEP meeting instruction talked, started, and led their IEP meetings more than students who received teacher-directed IEP instruction. Woods et al. (2010) found that students who received instruction in transition planning had greater knowledge and perceived self-efficacy of transition planning than students who did not receive instruction. A variety of commercially available curricula have been used to teach students to direct their IEP meeting, including *Self-Advocacy Strategy* (Van Reusen, Bos, & Schumaker, 1994), *Whose Future Is It Anyway?* (Wehmeyer, Lawrence, Garner, Soukup, & Palmer, 2004), and *Self-Directed IEP* (Martin, Marshall, Maxson, & Jerman, 1996).

Using the *Self-Advocacy Strategy* (Van Reusen et al., 1994) curriculum to teach student participation in the IEP meeting is an evidence-based practice identified by the National Secondary Transition Technical Assistance Center (NSTTAC). The focus of this strategy is to teach students both the behaviors needed to communicate in an IEP meeting and steps to help the student lead their IEP meeting. See Table 5.6 for a description of the strategy. Figure 5.5 provides a research-to-practice lesson plan starter that uses this strategy to teach IEP meeting participation.

Annual Goals

Your goals shoud be challenging and realistic. What should you be able to **DO** by the end of next year? Goals should be clear and measurable, and they need to <u>match your needs</u>.

1. I will _____

   _____

2. I will _____

   _____

Objectives

These are the steps you will take toward reaching your goals. Be sure they are clear and measurable. You and your teachers and family should be able to tell, without a doubt, when you have met each of your objectives.

To accomplish my first goal...

1a. I will_____

1b. I will_____

1c. I will_____

1d. I will_____

To accomplish my second goal...

2a. I will_____

2b. I will_____

2c. I will_____

2d. I will_____

Figure 5.3. Sample individualized education program template.

From Konrad, M., & Test, D.W. (2004). Teaching middle-school students with disabilities to use an IEP template. *Career Development for Exceptional Individuals, 27,* 101–124; reprinted by permission.

In *Evidence-Based Instructional Strategies for Transition* by David W. Test.
(2012, Paul H. Brookes Publishing Co., Inc.)

GO 4 IT...NOW!

Use the top part of this worksheet to do your prewriting.

Goal _____

Objectives

4 (4 objectives)   1. _____

2. _____

3. _____

4. _____

Identify

Timeline   _____

Name your topic.

Order your details.

Wrap it up and restate topic.

Remember to use the transition words pyramid!

First

Then   Second

Then   Next   Third

Then   Last   Finally   Fourth

_____

_____

_____

Figure 5.4. *GO 4 IT...NOW!* worksheet.

From Konrad, M., & Test, D.W. (2007). GO 4 IT...NOW! Unpublished form; reprinted by permission.

In *Evidence-Based Instructional Strategies for Transition* by David W. Test.
(2012, Paul H. Brookes Publishing Co., Inc.)

Table 5.6. The *Self-Advocacy Strategy* behaviors

Meeting strategy (IPARS)

  I   Inventory listing strengths, weaknesses, needs, and goals that is completed before the meeting

  P Provide the inventory during the meeting.

  A Ask questions.

  R Respond to questions.

  S Summarize the goals.

Source: Van Reusen, Bos, and Schumaker (1994).

Using *Self-Directed IEP* (Martin et al., 1996) to teach IEP meeting participation is also an evidence-based practice that uses multimedia to teach students to lead their IEP meeting. This curriculum consists of a video of a student who models each step, a student workbook, and a teacher's manual. See Table 5.7 for a list of the 11 steps to leading an IEP meeting. Figure 5.6 provides a research-to-practice lesson plan starter on using the *Self-Directed IEP* to teach IEP meeting participation.

Wu, Martin, and Isbell (2007) taught students with visual impairments to lead their IEP meetings using Self-Directed IEP. In addition, they trained the other IEP meeting participants about student-led IEPs. These students talked more at their meeting—and led more of it—than did students who led meetings in which the other participants did not receiving training on student-led IEPs.

Implementing the Plan

The final stage in the IEP process is student implementation of the written IEP. This phase involves teaching strategies to students to assist them with meeting their IEP goals. During this time, students should be taught how to set a goal, work toward that goal, monitor their progress, and make any changes that are necessary to meet their goals. The Self-Determined Learning Model of Instruction (SDLMI), *Take Action: Making Goals Happen*, and self-determination contracts can all be used to help students implement their IEPs.

The SDLMI is an instructional method used to teach students to set a goal, make a plan to reach that goal, and adjust the goal or plan based on actions (Wehmeyer, Palmer, Agran, Mithaug, & Martin, 2000). Using this model to teach students about educational goal attainment has been identified as an evidence-based practice by NSTTAC. In this method, students answer a series of questions designed to assist them with setting and attaining goals (see Table 5.8).

Goal setting and attainment is a life-long skill that students should learn. In one study (Agran, Blanchard, & Wehmeyer, 2000), high school students were taught to attain their IEP goals using the SDLMI. Almost all of the students increased performance on their self-selected goals.

The *Take Action: Making Goals Happen* curriculum consists of four steps: plan, act, evaluate, and adjust (Marshall et al., 1999). Using this strategy, students are taught how to develop a plan to reach their daily goals, work toward their goals, evaluate their progress, and adjust their goals based on their evaluations (see Table 5.9). Figure 5.7 provides a research-to-practice lesson plan starter on teaching students to attain goals using *Take Action*.

IEP Meetings Participation

Using Self-Advocacy Strategy

Objective: To teach students to participate in their IEP

Setting: Taught in a high school setting

Materials: Used Inventory Sheets where students and their parents identify and list their perceptions of the student's learning strengths, weaknesses to improve, goals and interests, and preferences for classroom learning and studying

Content taught

The treatment intervention focuses on teaching the participants the IEP participant strategy (IPARS).

I	Inventory listing strengths, weaknesses, needs, and goals completed before the meeting
P	Provide inventory information during the IEP conference
A	Ask questions
R	Respond to questions
S	Summarize the IEP goals

These steps include such communication and social skills as active listening, using eye communication, having a pleasant tone of voice, using an open body posture, using statements to agree or disagree with what is being said, asking questions for clarification, responding to questions, using the Inventory Sheet to assist in presenting the information, and summarizing the goals that were agreed on by the conference participants.

Teaching procedures

1. *Orientation* provides an overview of the strategy.

2. *Describe* involves defining the IEP process, briefly describing the major behaviors associated with the strategy, and providing a rationale for each step in the strategy.

3. *Model and Prepare* involves the participants completing the Inventory Sheet and the teacher modeling each of the other steps in the strategy, eliciting good and bad examples of the behavior.

4. *Verbal Rehearsal* involves participants memorizing and elaborating on their understanding of the steps in the strategy and the associated behaviors.

5. *Strategy Practice and Feedback* involves giving participants a brief overview of the procedures and content of the IEP conference and participating in a simulated conference in which they respond to questions and statements typical of annual IEP conferences and provide feedback to each other.

Figure 5.5. Research-to-practice lesson plan starter for *Self-Advocacy Strategy*. (Key: IEP, individualized education program.)

(continued)

From National Secondary Transition Technical Assistance Center. (2008).
IEP meetings participation using Self-Advocacy Strategy. Charlotte, NC: Author.

In *Evidence-Based Instructional Strategies for Transition* by David W. Test.
(2012, Paul H. Brookes Publishing Co., Inc.)

6. *Generalization* stage involves having participants discuss when and how the strategy can be used in various types of conferences, and participating in a generalization session immediately preceding the student's scheduled IEP conference. During this 5-minute generalization session students review the steps in the strategy and their Inventory Sheets; they are given the opportunity to respond to several questions to "warm up" for the conference.

There are three types of training sessions: student sessions, a partner (parent and student) session, and a generalization session.

1. The student session consists of three 50-minute sessions on 3 consecutive days. These sessions occur during school hours with 3–5 students participating at one time. During these sessions, the student learns the strategies using the acquisition stages.

2. At the partner session, 2–4 students and their parents meet for approximately 2 hours outside school time. First the teacher and students describe the strategy to the parents, and the students assist their parents in completing the Inventory Sheet. Next, each student and his or her parent(s) review the information and "negotiate a partnership" by determining which goals are held in common and which goals are unique to the student or parent(s).

3. Finally, both the students and parents participate in a simulated conference. The generalization session is held immediately preceding the conference.

Method of evaluation

To determine the effectiveness of the intervention on student IEP conference participation, four dependent measures are collected:

1. Quantity of student goals identified on the Inventory Sheets

2. Quantity and quality of student verbal contributions during the IEP conference

3. Evaluation of student performance during the IEP conference, and

4. Conference length

Lesson plan based on
Van Reusen, A.K., & Bos, C.S. (1994). Facilitating student participation in individualized education programs through motivation strategy instruction. *Exceptional Children, 60,* 466–475.

From National Secondary Transition Technical Assistance Center. (2008).
IEP meetings participation using Self-Advocacy Strategy. Charlotte, NC: Author.

In *Evidence-Based Instructional Strategies for Transition* by David W. Test.
(2012, Paul H. Brookes Publishing Co., Inc.)

Table 5.7. Steps in the *Self-Directed IEP* curriculum

Begin the meeting by stating its purpose.

Introduce everyone at the meeting.

Review past goals and performance.

Ask for others' feedback.

State your school and transition goals.

Ask questions if you do not understand.

Deal with differences in opinion.

State the support you will need.

Summarize your goals.

Close the meeting by thanking everyone.

Work on goals all year.

From Martin, J.E., Marshall, L.H., Maxson, L.M., & Jerman, P.L. (1996). *The self-directed IEP* (p. 113). Longmont, CO: Sopris West; reprinted by permission, Cambium Learning Group-Sopris.

Key: IEP, individualized education program.

Similarly, self-determination contracts have been used to help students to plan, work, evaluate, and adjust their work on classroom activities (Martin et al., 2003). Using worksheets, students plan their day by deciding when they will work on particular activities, how much of these activities they will complete, and points they will earn for completing the activities correctly. (The points are used as a reward for the students.) Once students begin work on their activities, they track their completion in the same manner. The students then evaluate their work by determining if they began and ended on time, completed as much of the activity as they planned, and earned the planned number of points. The final phase is to have students make adjustments for the following day based on their current evaluation. See Figure 5.8 for a sample contract.

SUMMARY

Teaching students to be involved in transition planning is a year-round process. Students should be involved in all phases of their IEP process, including determining strengths, weaknesses, postsecondary outcomes, IEP goals, and services needed to help them achieve their goals; participating and leading their IEP meeting; and working on achieving their goals. Several commercially available and educator-made curricula are available to assist with teaching students these skills.

FOR FURTHER INFORMATION

National Longitudinal Transition Study 2 (www.nlts2.org)

Provides databases and reports on post-school outcomes for students with disabilities

Evidence-based Practices (www.nsttac.org/ebp/ExecsummaryPPs.pdf)

Identifies evidence-based practices in relationship to Kohler's five areas of transition programming: student-focused planning, student development, family involvement, program structure, and interagency collaboration

IEP Meeting Participation

Using ChoiceMaker Self-Directed IEP

Objective: To teach students to participate in IEP meetings through the use of *ChoiceMaker Self-Directed IEP* multimedia package that was modified for nonreaders

Setting: Self-contained high school classroom

Materials: *ChoiceMaker Self-Directed IEP* Multimedia Package (includes teacher's manual, student workbook, two videos). To obtain SD-IEP, call Sopris West Inc. at 1-800-547-6747. Cost: $120

Content taught

4 instructional units including

Instructional unit 1: Leading meeting
    Step 1: Begin meeting by stating a purpose
    Step 2: Introduce everyone
    Step 3: Review past goals and performance
    Step 10: Close meeting by thanking everyone

Instructional unit 2: Reporting interests
    Step 5: State your school and transition goals

Instructional unit 3: Reporting skills
    Step 5: State your school and transition goals

Instructional unit 4: Reporting options
    Step 9: Summarize your goals

Teaching procedures

1. Within each step a format is followed:
    a. Review of prior steps, as needed
    b. Preview lesson content and instruction on new vocabulary used.
    c. Videotape material provides model and sample situations used for guided practice.
    d. Workbook activities (teacher reads aloud, writes on overhead, and leads class discussion in place of workbook activities when needed) used to practice each step
    e. Teacher demonstrates and students practice for real IEP meetings.

Figure 5.6.   Research-to-practice lesson plan starter for *ChoiceMaker Self-Directed IEP*. (*Key:* IEP, individualized education program.)

From National Secondary Transition Technical Assistance Center. (2008).
IEP meeting participation: Using ChoiceMaker Self-Directed IEP. Charlotte, NC: Author.

In *Evidence-Based Instructional Strategies for Transition* by David W. Test.
(2012, Paul H. Brookes Publishing Co., Inc.)

f. Brief student skill evaluation

g. Ask students to relate skills to other situations; wrap up.

h. Picture prompts for Steps 1, 2, and 3 for students with limited reading, writing, and cognitive skills

Evaluation

1. **Five mock IEP meetings.** After each instrumental unit is completed, a mock IEP meeting is held using the following format:

   a. **State the purpose of the meeting**

   Name of Student (NOS), why are we having this meeting today?

   b. **Introduce everyone**

   NOS, who is attending this meeting? (May point to self and other members of the meeting and say, "Who is that?/I am"?)

   c. **Review past performance and goals**

   NOS, do you think you have worked hard in school so far? What have you been working on?

   d. **Student interests**

   Great, NOS. Before we look at new goals, let's talk about your interests. This discussion will help determine your new goals.

   - What do you want to learn about in school?
   - We have visited several job sites. What do you think you want to do after you graduate from high school?
   - What are some of your personal interests? What sports do you like to play or activities do you like to participate in? (Probe if necessary by providing examples of sports, activities, etc.)
   - If you were going to live on your own or with a roommate, what daily living skills would you be interested in learning about?
   - After you graduate from high school, where do you want to live?
   - What community activities would you like to participate in?

   e. **Skills and limits**

   Ask student what skills they are strong in for each area and what skills they lack.

   f. **Options and goals**

   Ok, now we are going to write down several options for education (replace education with each of the areas). From these options we are going to write goals for each of the transition areas.

   - You have mentioned several school subjects that you are interested in. What other school subjects would you like to learn about? Repeat this format for all areas (use pictorial representations of the student's options if needed).
   - Now from your options we are going to determine goals for you to work on. Talk to student about reasonable goals.

   g. **Closing the meeting**

   Now that we have finished determining your goals, it's time to end the meeting.

   Let's review.

   NOS what are your new goals? Great job!

   NOS, would you please bring our meeting to a close? (Cue for student to shake hands and say thank you.)

(continued)

From National Secondary Transition Technical Assistance Center. (2008).
IEP meeting participation: Using ChoiceMaker Self-Directed IEP. Charlotte, NC: Author.

In *Evidence-Based Instructional Strategies for Transition* by David W. Test.
(2012, Paul H. Brookes Publishing Co., Inc.)

h. Student performance in mock and real IEP meetings is measured using ChoiceMaker Curriculum Checklist:

Instructional units | **Skills measured**

Leading meeting
1. Begins meeting by stating a purpose
2. Introduces participants
3. Reviews past goals and performance
4. Closes meeting by summarizing decisions

Reporting interests
1. Expresses educations interests (e.g., clubs, classes, sports, academics)
2. Expresses employment interests (e.g., jobs, careers)
3. Expresses personal interests (e.g., health, relationships, recreation)
4. Expresses daily living interests (e.g., cooking, transportation)
5. Expresses housing interests (e.g., group home, independent living, supervised apartments)
6. Expresses community participation interests (e.g., sports, clubs)

Reporting skills
1. Expresses education skills
2. Expresses education limits
3. Expresses employment skills
4. Expresses employment limits
5. Expresses personal skills
6. Expresses personal limits
7. Expresses daily living skills
8. Expresses daily living limits
9. Expresses housing skills
10. Expresses housing limits
11. Expresses communication participation skills
12. Expresses communication participation limits

Reporting options
1. Indicates education options
2. Chooses education goals
3. Indicates employment options
4. Chooses employment goals
5. Indicates personal options
6. Chooses personal goals
7. Indicates daily living options
8. Chooses daily living goals
9. Indicates housing options
10. Chooses housing options
11. Indicates community participation options
12. Chooses community participation goals

From National Secondary Transition Technical Assistance Center. (2008). *IEP meeting participation: Using ChoiceMaker Self-Directed IEP.* Charlotte, NC: Author.

In *Evidence-Based Instructional Strategies for Transition* by David W. Test. (2012, Paul H. Brookes Publishing Co., Inc.)

i. **Real IEP meetings.** First real IEP meeting is before any instruction begins; second IEP meeting is held after all instruction and mock IEP meetings are completed.

1. _____, do you know why we are here today? Please tell us.

2. _____, please introduce the people attending your meeting.

3. Let's look at past goals and your progress towards them. (Cue for student to tell how well he did meeting past goals.)

4. Ok, before we get started, let's talk about your interests, _____. Is there anything you would like to learn about in school?

5. What do you want to do after you graduate?

6. What are some skills that you would need to have to learn, live, or work on your own?

7. What are some skills limits?

8. (Done before meeting.) I see you have some options for each transition area. Please tell us a few.

9. Great. Now let's decide on a goal for you to work towards. (Cue for student to state goal in each transition area.)

10. Nice job. Let's finish signing all of the paperwork and then we will end this meeting. Now that we've finished signing the papers, _____,

11. What are some goals you are going to work towards? Thank you. (Cue for student to say thanks and shake hands.)

Lesson plan based on

Allen, S., Smith, A., Test, D., Flowers, C., & Wood, W. (2002). The effects of self-directed IEP on student participation in IEP meetings. *Career Development for Exceptional Individuals, 24,* 107–120.

From National Secondary Transition Technical Assistance Center. (2008).
IEP meeting participation: Using ChoiceMaker Self-Directed IEP. Charlotte, NC: Author.

In *Evidence-Based Instructional Strategies for Transition* by David W. Test.
(2012, Paul H. Brookes Publishing Co., Inc.)

Table 5.8. Phases of the Self-Determined Learning Model of Instruction

Phases	Student questions
Phase 1: Set a goal	
What is my goal?	What do I want to learn?
	What do I know about it now?
	What must change for me to learn what I do not know?
	What can I do to make this happen?
Phase 2: Take action	
What is my plan?	What can I do to learn what I do not know?
	What could keep me from taking action?
	What can I do to remove these barriers?
	When will I take action?
Phase 3: Adjust goal or plan	
What have I learned?	What actions have I taken?
	What barriers have been removed?
	What has changed about what I do not know?
	Do I know what I want to know?

Source: Wehmeyer, Palmer, Agran, Mithaug, and Martin (2000).

PACER Center, ALLIANCE National Parent Technical Assistance Center (www.pacer.org/tatra/resources/transitionemp.asp)

Provides information to parents about transition planning and how to be involved in their children's education

TAKE CHARGE for the Future (Powers et al., 2001)

Curriculum to teach students about the transition planning process, help students identify goals, and assist students with developing plans to reach their goals

IEP Template (Konrad & Test, 2004)

A template to help students develop their present level of performance, goals and objectives, and services needed to achieve their goals

GO FOR IT...NOW! (Konrad & Test, 2007)

A self-regulated writing strategy to teach students to write IEP goal paragraphs

Steps to Self-Determination (Hoffman & Field, 2005)

A curriculum to teach self-determination skills to students with disabilities

Table 5.9. *Take Action: Making Goals Happen* student questions

Strategy	What methods will I use?
Support	What help do I need?
Schedule	When will I do it?

Source: Marshall, Martin, Maxson, Miller, McGill, Hughes, and Jerman (1999).

IEP Daily Goal Attainment

Objective: To teach adolescent students with mild to moderate mental disabilities to attain their daily IEP goals

Setting: Teach in classroom setting

Materials: Instructional material is *Take Action: Making Goals Happen* (Marshall, Martin, Maxson, Miller, McGill, Hughes, & Jerman, 1999; available from Sopris West)

Content taught

Use the daily goal attainment format from *Take Action: Making Goals Happen*.

1. The students answer three questions to accomplish their daily plan:
   Strategy: What methods will I use?
   Support: What help do I need?
   Schedule: When will I do it?
   Students learn to evaluate and adjust their plans daily instead of weekly.

2. Depending upon the student's acquisition speed, teaching requires 6–10 hours of instruction across 1–2 weeks. With the daily goal format students don't break long-term goals into short-term objectives, but rather use goals that can be accomplished daily.

3. Based on student IEPs, the classroom teacher makes 30 daily goal cards for each student representing a broad range of tasks that each could perform, but have not yet mastered at a fluent or maintenance level. Each goal is printed on a 3" x 5" white note card. Example daily goals include
   a) Having a bus pass in a pocket or backpack
   b) Taking a recipe box to home economics cooking class
   c) Locating five items on a grocery list at the supermarket
   d) Finding the want ad section in the daily newspaper
   e) Not interrupting a conversation
   f) Making scrambled eggs
   g) Finding the movie section in the newspaper
   h) Doing five tasks in a row without a prompt

(continued)

Figure 5.7. Research-to-practice lesson plan starter for *Take Action: Making Goals Happen.* (Key: IEP, individualized education program.)

From National Secondary Transition Technical Assistance Center. (2008). *IEP daily goal attainment.* Charlotte, NC: Author.

In *Evidence-Based Instructional Strategies for Transition* by David W. Test.
(2012, Paul H. Brookes Publishing Co., Inc.)

Teaching procedure

In a 3-week period, the *Take Action* lessons are used to teach daily goal attainment. Students are taught the *Take Action* lessons during four 90-minute classes.

Class 1: Students complete a series of activities to learn the four steps of the Take Action process: plan, act, evaluate, and adjust.

Class 2: Students watch the Take Action video. The teacher also teaches the three plan components: strategy, scheduling, and support.

Class 3: Students interactively review sample plans, write practice plans, and develop plans to accomplish their own goals.

Class 4: Students learn evaluation strategies to determine if their strategy, support, and schedule achieved their goal. If not, students learn to adjust their plan parts to attain their goal.

1. Throughout instruction, at the start of each school day, the students choose three goals from their individualized stack of 30 goal cards. They read them, and if needed, the teacher helps them read. The students have one full school day to attain these goals.

2. Following instruction, students practice using the Take Action process to attain their daily goals for up to six days. Students complete their Take Action plans with teacher prompts and feedback, then work on attaining their goals while receiving teacher prompts and feedback. At the end of the day, the students complete the evaluation and adjustment sections with teacher support, instruction, and feedback.

Method of evaluation

Record the number of daily goals attained out of three daily goals chosen by the student.

Lesson plan based on

German, S.L., Martin, J.E., Marshall, L.H., & Sale, P.R. (2000). Promoting self-determination: Using *Take Action* to teach goal attainment. *Career Development for Exceptional Individuals, 23,* 27–38.

From National Secondary Transition Technical Assistance Center. (2008). *IEP daily goal attainment.* Charlotte, NC: Author.

In *Evidence-Based Instructional Strategies for Transition* by David W. Test.
(2012, Paul H. Brookes Publishing Co., Inc.)

Self-Determination Contract

Name: _____   Date: _____

Page #: _____   Problem #: _____

_____ I read my last adjustment statements.

Plan

Time began	Schedule	Subject	Objectives			Time end	Approval
(clock)	_____	Reading	page # _____	# correct _____	# points _____	(clock)	_____
(clock)	_____	Math	# problems _____	# correct _____	# points _____	(clock)	_____
(clock)	_____	Spelling	# words _____	# correct _____	# points _____	(clock)	_____
(clock)	_____	Creative	story # _____		# points _____	(clock)	_____
(clock)	_____	Social	# events _____		# points _____	(clock)	_____

Work

Time began	Schedule	Subject	Objectives			Time end	Approval
(clock)	_____	Reading	page # _____	# correct _____	# points earned _____	(clock)	_____
(clock)	_____	Math	# problems _____	# correct _____	# points earned _____	(clock)	_____

Figure 5.8. Self-determination contract.

(continued)

From Martin, J.E., Mithaug, D.E., Cox, P., Peterson, L.Y., Van Dycke, J.L., & Cash, M.E. (2003). Increasing self-determination: Teaching students to plan, work, evaluate, and adjust. *Exceptional Children, 69,* 431–447; reprinted by permission.

In *Evidence-Based Instructional Strategies for Transition* by David W. Test.
(2012, Paul H. Brookes Publishing Co., Inc.)

Self-Determination Contract (continued)

_____ Spelling # words ____ # correct ____ # points earned ____ _____
____

_____ Creative story # _____ # points earned ____ _____
____

_____ Social # events _____ # points earned ____ _____
____

Evaluate

	Reading	Math	Spelling	Writing	Social
Began on time?	Yes No	Yes No	Yes No	Yes No	Yes No
Completed planned number?	Yes No	Yes No	Yes No	Yes No	Yes No
Completed planned number correctly?	Yes No	Yes No	Yes No	Yes No	Yes No
Earned planned number of points?	Yes No	Yes No	Yes No	Yes No	Yes No
Ended on time?	Yes No	Yes No	Yes No	Yes No	Yes No

Adjust

Next time	Reading	Math	Spelling	Writing	Social
Begin work:					
Earlier	_____	_____	_____	_____	_____
Later	_____	_____	_____	_____	_____
Same time	_____	_____	_____	_____	_____
Complete:					
More pages/problems	_____	_____	_____	_____	_____
Same number pages/problems	_____	_____	_____	_____	_____
Work _____ number of problems/pages correctly:					
More	_____	_____	_____	_____	_____
Same	_____	_____	_____	_____	_____
Earn _____ number of points:					
More	_____	_____	_____	_____	_____
Same	_____	_____	_____	_____	_____
End work:					
Earlier	_____	_____	_____	_____	_____
Later	_____	_____	_____	_____	_____

From Martin, J.E., Mithaug, D.E., Cox, P., Peterson, L.Y., Van Dycke, J.L., & Cash, M.E. (2003). Increasing self-determination: Teaching students to plan, work, evaluate, and adjust. *Exceptional Children, 69*, 431–447; reprinted by permission.

In *Evidence-Based Instructional Strategies for Transition* by David W. Test.
(2012, Paul H. Brookes Publishing Co., Inc.)

Lesson Plan Starters

Person-Centered Planning (http://www.nsttac.org/LessonPlanLibrary/2_27_35.pdf)

Self-Advocacy Strategy (http://www.nsttac.org/LessonPlanLibrary/6.pdf; http://www.nsttac.org/
   LessonPlanLibrary/4_7_37_41.pdf; http://www.nsttac.org/LessonPlanLibrary/5.pdf)

Self-Directed IEP (http://www.nsttac.org/LessonPlanLibrary/1_and_8.pdf)

Take Action: Making Goals Happen (http://www.nsttac.org/LessonPlanLibrary/26.pdf)

6

Student Development: Employment Skills

Allison Walker and Audrey Bartholomew

Since the mid-1980s, improving the employment rate of students with disabilities has been a focus of research as practitioners and researchers began investigating better ways to prepare students for the world of work. According to Kohler and Field (2003), one of the ways to better prepare students for the world of work is to build students' work-related skills through school-based and work-based activities. In this process, practitioners should identify the accommodations and supports students would need to be successful, as well as teach these skills across multiple settings. By teaching the skills across multiple settings (including school-based and community-based settings), students are more likely to generalize the skills to other environments and therefore be successful in the world of work.

Kohler and Field (2003) described the use of teaching work-related skills through school and work-based activities as part of the student development component of Kohler's Taxonomy for Transition Programming.

Researchers in the mid-1980s built a foundation for later studies, such as Kohler and Field (2003), by examining the poor post-school outcomes of students with disabilities. For example, in a follow-up study of 234 high school graduates who completed special education services in 1978, Mithaug, Horiuchi, and Fanning (1985) found that 82% of these students had held a job at one time since graduation. However, results also showed that in the first year after graduation, the average number of jobs held by a respondent was 3.1. In addition, 29% of students found the jobs themselves, whereas 16% received help from a teacher and 13% received help from friends. Results did not show that respondents received help from parents or relatives.

Similarly, Hasazi, Gordon, and Roe (1985) studied 462 youth with disabilities who exited high school between 1979 and 1983 from nine Vermont school districts. They found that 65% of these individuals were employed; 83% of them found jobs on their own or with help from family or friends. Results from this study also indicated the need for educational and vocational experiences (e.g., vocational education, work experience program, part-time and summer jobs during high school) to help students obtain employment after high school. Halpern (1985) echoed the need for vocational education in the transition programming of students with disabilities at the secondary level by requiring career education for all students receiving special education services.

The emphasis on teaching employment skills to students at the secondary level continued in later studies, which helped contribute to the improvement of the employment status of students with disabilities since the 1980s (Benz et al., 2000; Benz, Yovanoff, & Doren, 1997). The National Longitudinal Transition Study 2 (NLTS2) tracked this improvement by examining a sample of students with disabilities across the nation who were 13–16 years old and receiving special education services in the 2000–2001 school year. Results of students' employment status showed that 72% of students with disabilities were employed at some point after leaving high school. However, at the time of the NLTS2 interview, only 57% were employed, which shows variation in their employment status. Data on the average number of jobs held by youth with disabilities from the NLTS2 study is similar to the results found in the Mithaug, Horiuchi, and Fanning (1985) study. NLTS2 found that youth with disabilities held two to three jobs within the first 4 years after high school. Despite the steady increase in employment rate for students with disabilities, there remains a need for teaching employment skills and using evidence-based practices at the secondary level to decrease the variation in employment status and improve the employment outcomes of students with disabilities. This need has been recognized by the National Career Technical Education Foundation in their development of "career clusters." The purpose of these career clusters is to merge academic and occupational skills into courses that meet the demanding needs in the workplace so that students can make a smooth transition into the workforce. Several of the career clusters are described in this chapter and how they relate to the evidence-based practices used at the secondary level.

The NLTS2 focused "on a wide range of important topics, such as high school coursework, extracurricular activities, academic performance, postsecondary education and training, employment, independent living, and community participation" (National Center for Special Education Research, 2005).

According to the literature database developed by the National Secondary Transition Technical Assistance Center (NSTTAC), several practices related to teaching employment skills have been identified as evidence based. NSTTAC specifically found that job-specific employment skills could be taught using least-to-most prompting, self-management, computer-assisted instruction (CAI), community-based instruction (CBI), and response prompting. Findings also showed that mnemonics can be used to effectively teach students with disabilities how to complete a job application. Each of these practices will be described in this chapter to show the evidence base and how they were implemented in previous research.

LEAST-TO-MOST PROMPTING

According to Cooper, Heron, and Heward (2007), least-to-most prompting is a method used to transfer stimulus control from response prompts to the natural stimulus when a participant does not respond to the natural stimulus or makes an incorrect response. This strategy begins with the interventionist providing the least amount of assistance in each trial. If the participant does not provide the correct response, the interventionist increases the level of assistance with each successive trial. For example, least-to-most prompting can be used to teach a student how to press a switch to activate a verbal command:

1. The first level of prompting should be a verbal prompt from the interventionist requesting the student to press the switch.

2. If the student does not press the switch, the interventionist may gesture to the student by pointing to the switch.

3. If the student still does not press the switch, the interventionist can model how to press the switch by actually pressing the switch.

4. If the student still does not press the switch, the interventionist can perform a partial physical prompt by gently touching the back of the student's arm and pushing it toward the switch.

5. If the student still has not pressed the switch, the "most" level of assistance should be provided by using hand-over-hand assistance, in which the interventionist can put his or her hand over the student's hand and simultaneously press the switch.

Researchers have used least-to-most prompting in the classroom and community to teach specific employment skills. For example, Bates, Cuvo, Miner, and Korabek (2001) combined least-to-most prompting with CBI and social praise to teach cleaning a restroom. In addition, Smith, Collins, Schuster, and Kleinert (1999) used least-to-most prompting with multiple exemplars and a continuous reinforcement schedule to teach cleaning tables.

According to the States' Career Cluster Initiative (SCCI), students in grades 9–12 are required to complete training, education, and certification to prepare for employment in a particular field. Therefore, practitioners can meet this skill by using least-to-most prompting to help students interpret the information presented to them along with the prompts while learning the skills needed to perform specific job skills.

Using least-to-most prompting also relates to Indicator 13 because least-to-most prompting can be used as a transition service to teach specific job skills. According to Indicator 13, a transition service includes instruction, related service, community experience, or development of employment and other post-school adult living objectives and (if appropriate) acquisition of daily living skills and provision of a functional vocational evaluation. Therefore, when practitioners are developing a transition plan for a student, it would be appropriate to incorporate least-to-most prompting into the transition plan as a form of instruction to teach specific employment skills.

To incorporate least-to-most prompting as a form of instruction into a lesson plan, practitioners can use the information found in studies such as Smith et al. (1999). However, some practitioners may not have access to these studies or know how to interpret the information presented in these journal articles. Therefore, NSTTAC has analyzed many evidence-based practices published in peer-reviewed journals to give practitioners user-friendly lesson plans describing how these practices can be implemented across settings. Figure 6.1 provides a research-to-practice lesson plan starter based on the study by Smith et al. This lesson plan includes step-by-step teaching procedures on the use of least-to-most prompting to teach students with disabilities how to perform a job-specific skill (e.g., cleaning a table).

COMMUNITY-BASED INSTRUCTION

CBI is a form of instruction in which the community serves as the classroom (Kluth, 2000). The purpose of CBI is to teach students functional skills in natural environments (Hamill, 2002). That is, instruction occurs in settings that are practical and facilitate meaningful experiences so that students can practice skills in places they would most likely use them.

Using Least-to-Most Prompting to Teach a Specific Job Skill

Cleaning a Table

Objective: To teach students to clean a table

Settings: The one-to-one instruction is conducted within a kitchen area

Materials: Materials included buckets and cloths of different shapes and colors. The tables used were also different shapes and colors. Soap and water was also included.

Content taught

Students are taught how to clean a table with multiple examples of materials and tables by color and shape.

Preparing materials task analysis:
1. Walk to cabinet
2. Open cabinet door
3. Take out bucket
4. Set bucket on counter
5. Take out soap
6. Pour soap into container
7. Put soap into bucket
8. Turn on water
9. Set bucket under water
10. Turn water off at proper level
11. Set bucket on counter
12. Open cabinet door
13. Take out cloth
14. Place cloth in bucket
15. Close cabinet door

Cleaning table task analysis:
1. Place bucket on another table
2. Pick up cloth
3. Place cloth in soap and water
4. Wring out cloth
5. Rub section one of table
6. Place cloth in bucket
7. Wring out cloth
8. Rub section two of table
9. Place cloth in bucket
10. Wring out cloth
11. Rub section three of table
12. Place cloth in bucket

Figure 6.1. Research-to-practice lesson plan starter for using least-to-most prompting to teach the specific job skill of cleaning a table.

From National Secondary Transition Technical Assistance Center. (2008). *Cleaning a table.* Charlotte, NC: Author.

In *Evidence-Based Instructional Strategies for Transition* by David W. Test.
(2012, Paul H. Brookes Publishing Co., Inc.)

Putting away materials task analysis:

1. Pick up bucket
2. Take bucket to sink
3. Take cloth out of bucket
4. Turn on water
5. Rinse out cloth
6. Pour water down drain
7. Rinse out bucket
8. Turn off water
9. Place cloth on bucket
10. Open cabinet door
11. Place bucket in cabinet
12. Close soap container
13. Place soap in cabinet
14. Close cabinet door

Teaching procedures

1. Teacher will demonstrate steps of the cleaning table task analysis one time.

2. Teacher will provide instruction one-to-one in the classroom using total task format.

3. Teacher will initially use verbal praise as a consequence for correct responses on a continuous schedule of reinforcement.

4. Following one day at criterion, teacher will fade reinforcement to a fixed ratio of 6 for one day then to a fixed ratio of 12 schedule for one day.

5. The teacher will provide an opportunity for observational learning at the beginning and end of each instructional session while preparing or putting away materials.

6. At the beginning of the session, the teacher will cue the target that they are beginning by stating, "We need to get our materials ready to clean the tables."

7. As the teacher prepares the materials, allow each student to watch while verbally explaining the process.

8. At the end of the session, the teacher will state, "We need to put away our materials" and again describe each step in the sequence while the students watch.

Evaluation

Collect data on percent correct of steps completed independently on the three separate task analyses.

Lesson plan based on

Smith, R.L., Collins, B.C., Schuster, J.W., & Kleinert, H. (1999). Teaching table cleaning skills to secondary students with moderate/severe disabilities: Facilitating observational learning during instructional downtime. *Education and Training in Mental Retardation and Developmental Disabilities, 34,* 342–353.

Research has indicated one way to teach employment skills is by using CBI. For example, Bates, Cuvo, Miner, and Korabek (2001) combined CBI with simulated instruction to teach cleaning a public restroom. Additionally, Cihak, Alberto, Kessler, and Taber (2004) also used a combination of CBI with simulated instruction to teach using a copy machine and collating a newsletter. Finally, DiPipi-Hoy, Jitendra, and Kern (2009) used CBI to teach time management skills at community employment settings. Figure 6.2 provides a research-to-practice lesson plan starter on using CBI to teach the specific job skill of making and collating photocopies.

Some skills that have been taught using community-based instruction include purchasing, pedestrian safety, riding a bus, and community social skills (Beakley & Yoder, 1998; Burcroff, Radogna, & Wright, 2003; Kluth, 2000).

Indicator 13 requires students to have postsecondary employment goals and supporting annual goals. Educators can use CBI as an instructional method to help students acquire employment skills while in school to make progress toward their postsecondary employment goals. In addition, instruction provided on the jobsite can be listed as a transition service on the individualized education program (IEP) and information about student performance at work can add to their transition assessment.

Using CBI to teach employment skills is also aligned with the SCCI. For example, instruction in community-based employment can help students gain skills to acquire a job, which is one of the standards included in the SCCI. Additionally and more specifically, the research that supports the practice of using CBI to teach employment skills includes teaching individuals how to clean a restroom. This skill can be valuable to students pursuing employment within the hospitality/tourism and business/business administration clusters. Cleaning a restroom can also be aligned with a general skill that cuts across clusters, such as maintaining clean restrooms to ensure the facility is in compliance with health and safety codes. Examples from the supporting research for the practice also include using a copy machine, which is another general skill that cuts across clusters.

SELF-MANAGEMENT

Self-management involves proactive strategies used to change or maintain one's own behavior. It has commonly been used to teach students how to regulate their own behaviors and deter inappropriate classroom behaviors (Rafferty, 2010). However, research has shown that self-management behaviors can be used to teach additional behaviors, such as job-specific skills (Lancioni & O'Reilly, 2001).

Self-management has been used with students with intellectual disabilities who are 14–21 years old to teach job-specific skills. This practice involves a variety of strategies, including teaching students to use picture cues on cards, picture cues stored in computer-aided systems, object cues, verbal cues stored in recording devices, and self-verbalizations. Each of these strategies may deliver prompts for individuals to follow either a task analysis or schedule of activities at work. For example, an individual may be presented with a task analysis to complete a task at work in the form of pictures they must visually inspect and follow. Individuals may also use picture cues to follow a schedule of activities for the workday.

Using self-management to promote employment skills is related to both Indicator 13 and national standards. Employment, in general, should be included in a student's IEP as a postsecondary goal. For example, a possible postsecondary goal may read *Lisa will obtain part-time employment working in a pet store*. In addition, self-management as a practice can be written as an annual goal and/or transition service that supports the postsecondary goal. For

Using Community-Based Instruction to Teach Job-Specific Skills

Objective: To teach students to make collated photocopies using simulated and community based instruction on the same day

Setting:

1. Simulated instruction: Classroom
2. Community instruction: Local print shop

Materials:

1. Copy machine with top feeder tray and keypad
2. Camera to take photographs of photocopy machine
3. Photo album

For each of 9 steps in the task analysis, create four photographs that correspond to step (i.e., a total of 48 photographs) including:

- 1 photograph depicting correct action being performed in the relevant setting
- 1 photograph depicting correct materials, but wrong manipulation
- 1 photograph depicting an out of sequence action
- 1 photograph depicting an action associated with the task, but not included in the training sequence

A photo of the discriminative stimulus was on the page opposite the four photos (e.g., Please select card type.)

Content taught

Task analysis:

1. Place the original newsletter on the feeder tray.
2. Enter a four-digit personal identification number (PIN) code.
3. Press the ID button.
4. Press the number *5* for the number of copies.
5. Press the collate button.
6. Press the *ok* button.
7. Press the *start* button.
8. Remove the original from the upper tray.
9. Remove the copies from the bottom tray.

Figure 6.2. Research-to-practice lesson plan starter for using community-based instruction to teach job-specific skills. *(continued)*

From National Secondary Transition Technical Assistance Center. (2008). *Collating photocopies.* Charlotte, NC: Author.

In *Evidence-Based Instructional Strategies for Transition* by David W. Test.
(2012, Paul H. Brookes Publishing Co., Inc.)

Teaching procedures

1. On the same day, provide training in simulated settings approximately 3 hours before community-based instruction. For example, provide instruction using the simulated procedures on Monday morning and provide community-based instruction on Monday afternoon.

2. During simulated instruction, use the photo album to provide instruction.
   a. Tell students to pretend they are going to make copies using a photocopy machine.
   b. Present the photo album to the student.
   c. Tell students to visually scan the photos on the album cover and point to the picture indicating the task they would complete.
   d. Present task materials to the student.
   e. Open the album and ask, "What is the first thing you do?"
   f. Tell students to put a finger on the photo that depicts what is next on each photo page.
   g. Use a system of least prompts with a 3-second interval between each prompt level. To assist a student in successfully identifying the photos depicting steps to complete the task, prompts should be provided in the following order:
      • Verbal prompt (e.g., "Do you see where the writing is?")
      • Gesture (e.g., pointing to discriminative stimulus on page opposite the four photos)
      • Gesture plus verbal explanation (e.g., pointing to the discriminative stimulus on page opposite the 4 photos and providing a verbal explanation)
      • Modeling plus verbal explanation (e.g., pointing to correct picture and plus providing verbal explanation).
      • Physical assistance plus verbal explanation (e.g., holding the student's wrist, guiding the correct response, and providing an explanation)

3. Approximately 3 hours later, provide training at a photocopy machine in a community print shop.
   • Tell students that they are going to make copies using a photocopy machine.
   • Use a system of least prompts with a 3-second interval between each prompt level
   • To assist a student in successfully completing the task, prompts should be provided in the following order:
      a. Verbal prompt (e.g., "Do you see where the writing is?")
      b. Gesture (e.g., pointing to discriminative stimulus on the machine)
      c. Gesture plus verbal explanation (e.g., pointing to the discriminative stimulus and providing a verbal explanation
      d. Modeling plus verbal explanation (e.g., demonstrating appropriate actions plus verbal explanation)
      e. Physical assistance plus verbal explanation (e.g., holding the student's wrist, guiding the correct response, and providing an explanation)

Evaluation

Collect student performance data on the number of steps completed independently and correctly.

Lesson plan based on

Cihak, D.F., Alberto, P.A., Kessler, K., & Taber, T.A. (2004). An investigation of instructional scheduling arrangements for community based instruction. *Research in Developmental Disabilities, 25,* 67–88.

From National Secondary Transition Technical Assistance Center. (2008). *Collating photocopies.* Charlotte, NC: Author.

In *Evidence-Based Instructional Strategies for Transition* by David W. Test.
(2012, Paul H. Brookes Publishing Co., Inc.)

example, an annual goal listed on an IEP may read *Lisa will self-monitor her ability to arrive to work on time for five consecutive days with 90% accuracy.* A possible transition service would be instruction in self-determination skills such as self-management.

In addition to Indicator 13, some of the specific self-management strategies taught in the supporting research can be aligned with the college and career-ready common core standards. For example, reading a picture schedule can be aligned with the anchor standards for reading. The specific outcomes of the research in using self-management to teach job-specific skills can be aligned with the SCCI. For example, identifying and exploring career opportunities in one or more career pathways to build an understanding of job opportunities is identified as an essential skill that cuts across clusters.

COMPUTER-ASSISTED INSTRUCTION

CAI uses computers to teach skills such as language, communication, reading, math, and also functional skills such as job-specific employment skills. Technology-based supports in employment settings can be delivered through a variety of devices including laptop computers, smartphones, and digital music players to deliver audio prompting, picture cues (Cihak, Kessler, & Alberto, 2007), video cues (Van Laarhoven, Johnson, Van Laarhoven-Myers, Grider, & Grider, 2009), video modeling, and/or simulation activities (Mechling & Ortega-Hurndon, 2007), as well as a device that can be used to access software that is specifically designed or modified for the use of instruction for students with disabilities (Riffel et al., 2005).

CAI has a variety of benefits, including the following:

- It overcomes the problem of not being able to use real-life settings because of limited resources (e.g., staffing, time, money, transportation) by creating a more realistic learning environment than what the classroom has to offer (Wissick, Gardner, & Langone, 1999).
- It can be used in a variety of settings where instructional staff may not be available (e.g., home).
- It is often preferred by participants (Riffel et al., 2005).
- It can be implemented by a variety of staff members with a certain level of fidelity (Branham, Collins, Schuster, & Kleinert, 1999).

Using CAI to teach job-specific employment skills has been effective with students with mild and moderate intellectual disabilities, as well as a variety of ages ranging from 16 to 21 years. Along with a varied population, CAI has been used to teach an array of skills, such as setting cafeteria and dining room tables, rolling silverware, delivering office mail, watering plants, changing paper towels, and sorting office supplies. Figure 6.3 provides a research-to-practice lesson plan starter displaying instruction using a computer-based video (Mechling & Ortega-Hurndon, 2007) to teach job-specific skills to be used in the workplace.

Teaching job-specific employment skills using CAI is related to both Indicator 13 and national standards. Like self-management, CAI can be incorporated into both annual goals and transition services to support a postsecondary goal. For example, an annual goal listed on an IEP may read *Lisa will stay on task for at least 6 minutes while being provided with continual audio prompts for five consecutive days.* A possible transition service would be instruction using CAI, such as video modeling.

In addition to aligning with Indicator 13, using CAI to teach employment skills is also aligned with the college and career readiness common core standards for speaking and listening. For example, some of the supporting research for this practice includes audio

Using Computer-Based Instruction to Teach Job Skills

Objective: To teach students to water a plant, deliver mail, and change paper towels.

Setting: Instruction is conducted in a small office four times per week. Skill generalization is measured in the community at a job site.

Materials: Materials include a laptop computer, a PowerPoint computer software program, digital video camera, Windows Movie Maker, a CD-ROM, and a *Magic Touch* touchscreen. Materials for skill generalization include: a 24-inch canvas bag with a strap, plastic bottle filled with water, one roll of paper towels without plastic wrapping, an empty roll of paper towels, and a legal size envelope.

Content taught

Photograph on computer screen	Video recording of task analysis
Job skill 1: Watering a plant	
Elevator	Walk to elevator
Inside elevator floor panel	Touch 3
Scene to left of elevator on 3rd floor	Turn, walk to left
Plant	Walk to plant
Water bottle	Water plant
Job Skill 2: Delivering mail	
Elevator	Walk to elevator
Inside elevator floor panel	Touch 2
Scene to left of elevator on 2nd floor	Turn, walk to left
Table in office	Walk to table
Envelope on table	Put envelope in bag
Elevator	Walk to elevator
Outside elevator *up/down* panel	Touch *down* arrow
Inside elevator floor panel	Touch *1*
Counter on 1st floor	Walk to counter
Envelope on counter	Put envelope on counter
Job Skill: Changing paper towels	
Restroom door	Walk to restroom
Empty roll of paper towels	Put empty roll of paper towels in bag
Full roll of paper towels	Put full roll of paper towels on top of cabinet
Classroom door	Walk to classroom door

Figure 6.3.   Research-to-practice lesson plan starter for using computer-based instruction to teach job skills.

From National Secondary Transition Technical Assistance Center. (2008). *Job skills using computer based instruction.* Charlotte, NC: Author.

In *Evidence-Based Instructional Strategies for Transition* by David W. Test.
(2012, Paul H. Brookes Publishing Co., Inc.)

Teaching procedures

1. Prior to the lesson
   a. Create video recordings with sound and digital still photographs of each step of task analysis for each job task (e.g., watering a plant, delivering mail, changing paper towels in a restroom).
      i. The teacher will create video recordings of task analysis using a subjective point of view (move the camera as if it were the student and show what the student would be seeing).
      ii. Video will show the instructor completing each step of the task analysis.
      iii. Video should be recorded separately and edited using Windows Movie Maker, and saved on CD-ROM.
   b. A *Magic Touch* touchscreen will be used to select photographs.
   c. Photographs should be hyperlinked (correct) to digital video clips that automatically play the step of the task analysis corresponding to the photograph.
   d. Program PowerPoint to advance to the next slide (touch of the computer screen), which will automatically play the video recording.
   e. Once the video stops, program PowerPoint to advance to the next slide containing 3 still photographs.
   f. Program PowerPoint to remain on this slide until the correct photograph corresponding to the next step in the task analysis is chosen.
2. Computer based video instruction
   a. Teacher will gain students' attention by directing the use of the touchscreen to make selections, and saying, "It's time to practice watering the plant, delivering mail, and changing paper towels on the computer."
   b. Students will be presented with three different photographs on the computer screen.
   c. The student will select (touch the screen) the one that corresponds to the next step of the task analysis to complete the job task.
   d. Once student provides correct response, a video recording showing completion of the task analysis step will be presented.
   e. Using a constant time delay procedure, begin with a 0-second delay until the student has 100% correct wait responses (correct response after teacher prompt) for one session.
   f. Then, use a 3-second constant time delay for all remaining instructional sessions.
   g. If the student provides an unprompted or prompted correct response, the computer program will advance to the next slide and will show a video recording of the next step of the task analysis.
   h. If the student provides an unprompted incorrect response, the teacher will point to the correct photograph.
   i. If the student provides a prompted incorrect or not response, the teacher will touch the correct photograph and advance the slide to the video screen.

Evaluation

Collect data on the number of correct student responses for the task analysis.

Lesson plan based on

Mechling, L.C., & Ortega-Hurndon, F. (2007). Computer-based video instruction to teach young adults with moderate intellectual disabilities to perform multiple step job tasks in a generalized setting. *Education and Training in Developmental Disabilities, 42*, 24–37.

prompting delivered by a computer. Additionally, many of the specific employment skills taught in the supporting research can be used to help students acquire post-school employment in some of the clusters identified in the SCCI. Finally, like the other practices discussed, CAI can help teach many of the required activities related to goal setting and monitoring, implementing personal safety rules, and exploring career opportunities.

MNEMONICS

According to Fontana, Scruggs, and Mastropieri (2007), mnemonic strategy instruction involves incorporating keywords to help students develop a better understanding of concrete information, which makes it more meaningful and easier to learn. Mnemonics is often used in combination with additional strategies to help students with memory difficulty learn and retain concepts.

Using mnemonics to teach students how to complete a job application has been identified as an evidence-based practice by the NSTTAC. Nelson, Smith, and Dodd (1994) used a mnemonic called *SELECT* to teach the steps of completing a job application:

Survey the entire application.

Emphasize words that indicate the type of information requested.

Locate cues that indicate where the information is to be entered.

Enter the information requested.

Check to see if the information is accurate.

Turn the application in to the appropriate individual.

The mnemonic was taught in combination with teacher-led discussion, introduction of strategy steps, modeling, verbal rehearsal, and independent practice. Figure 6.4 provides a research-to-practice lesson plan to teach students with disabilities how to use a mnemonic to complete a job application.

Mnemonics relates to Indicator 13 because the strategy can be written in an IEP objective or used as a transition service to help a student meet postsecondary independent living goals as a result of a transition assessment. In addition, using mnemonics integrates the SCCI knowledge of language as students use writing, speaking, reading, and listening skills to develop a concrete understanding of the concepts presented in the mnemonic. Finally, using mnemonics to teach job application skills is related to the college and career-ready common core standards. For example, filling out a job application requires students to evaluate information in diverse media and formats, including visually, as well as the use knowledge of language and its conventions when writing.

RESPONSE PROMPTING

According to Cooper et al. (2007), response prompting involves providing students with extra visual, auditory, textual, or symbolic prompts. These prompts then serve as extra cues and reminders for students to perform the desired behavior.

Response prompting is an evidence-based practice with a moderate level of evidence from two quality single-subject studies. These two studies implemented response prompting using static picture cues to teach initiation of job tasks, auditory prompts to teach how to clean a bathroom, and tactile cues to teach packaging skills. Figure 6.5 provides a

Using Mnemonics to Teach Completing a Job Application

Objective: To teach students to complete a job application

Setting: School classroom

Materials:

1. Entry level job applications
2. Job application information card containing this information:
   - Birth date
   - Social security number
   - Complete address
   - Telephone number
   - Educational experience
   - Previous work experience
   - References
   - Felony convictions (if applicable)
3. Overhead transparencies of job applications
4. Overhead transparencies of six step mnemonic called *SELECT*

Content taught

Students are taught to fill out a six-step job application using the mnemonic called SELECT.

The principle steps were sequenced into
1. **S**urvey the entire application.
2. **E**mphasize words that indicate the type of information requested.
3. **L**ocate cues that indicate where the information is to be entered
4. **E**nter the information requested.
5. **C**heck to see if the information is accurate.
6. **T**urn the application in to the appropriate individual.

Teaching procedures

1. Discuss goal of job application strategy (i.e., to help students accurately complete a job application) and why it is important to know how to accurately complete a job application.

2. Explain how they will be able to use the strategy whenever they apply for a job.

3. Overhead transparency is used to introduce and discuss six-step job application strategy until it is clear that students fully understand steps. This is accomplished through choral responding by students and informal checks by teacher.

Figure 6.4. Research-to-practice lesson plan starter for using mnemonics to teach completing a job application. *(continued)*

From National Secondary Transition Technical Assistance Center. (2008). *Job application completion.* Charlotte, NC: Author.

In *Evidence-Based Instructional Strategies for Transition* by David W. Test.
(2012, Paul H. Brookes Publishing Co., Inc.)

4. Model job application strategy with overhead transparency of job application by completing a standard job application while thinking out loud. To actively engage students, use prompts to encourage an interactive dialogue throughout demonstration, for example, "What is it I have to do? I need to . . ." and "How am I doing?" Students are encouraged to help teacher. After modeling, discuss the importance of using self-questioning statements while completing a job application.

5. Students are required to verbally practice job application strategy steps, including self-questioning statements, until they are memorized and students are able to do this correctly within a 15- to 20-minute rehearsal period.

6. Students are required to write down steps and associated self-questioning statements as they work through a job application. They are allowed to ask any questions and teacher provides corrective feedback only when asked by students throughout training session.

7. Ask students to complete a job application as if they are applying for an actual job. Explain that because there typically is no one there to help them complete job applications, they are to use only their job information card to complete the job application and that they have as much time as they need to complete the application.

8. Ask students to independently describe the steps they used to check whether they have employed the learning strategy.

Evaluation

Evaluate the student's performance by collecting data number of items correct on the job application.

Lesson plan based on

Nelson, J.R., Smith, D.J., & Dodd, J.M. (1994). The effects of learning strategy instruction on the completion of job applications by students. *Journal of Learning Disabilities, 27,* 104–110.

Using Response Prompting to Teach How to Clean a Bathroom Mirror, Sink, and Toilet

Objective: To teach students to clean a bathroom mirror, sink, and toilet

Setting: Instruction is conducted in a bathroom located in a classroom. Skill generalization is measured in a bathroom in the school's faculty lounge.

Materials: Materials include three small battery-operated portable cassette players with headphones, three separate cassettes for each student, bathroom cleaners, cleaning cloths, paper towels, toilet bowl brush, a wrist watch with a second hand, and reinforcers (e.g., self-selected cassettes of favorite music).

Content taught

Student is taught how to clean a bathroom mirror, sink, and toilet using a cassette player to provide an auditory prompt system with a fading component to teach the task analysis for each skill.

Task analysis for cleaning mirror:
1. Go to designated area
2. Get paper towel and cleaner
3. Spray cleaner on entire area
4. Wipe cleaner off
5. Throw paper towel away
6. Put cleaner away

Task analysis for cleaning sink:
1. Go to designated area
2. Wet cloth
3. Get wet cloth and cleaner
4. Spray cleaner on entire area
5. Wipe cleaner off
6. Hang up wet cloth to dry
7. Put cleaner away

Task analysis for cleaning toilet:
1. Go to designated area
2. Wet cloth
3. Get wet cloth and cleaner
4. Spray cleaner on entire outside area
5. Wipe cleaner off entire outside area
6. Hang up wet cloth to dry
7. Put cleaner away
8. Get bowl cleaner and brush
9. Squirt cleaner on entire inside bowl
10. Use brush to scrub the entire inside of the bowl
11. Put brush and cleaner away

Figure 6.5. Research-to-practice lesson plan starter for using response prompting to teach how to clean a bathroom mirror, sink, and toilet. *(continued)*

From National Secondary Transition Technical Assistance Center. (2008). *Cleaning bathroom mirror, sink, and toilet.* Charlotte, NC: Author.

In *Evidence-Based Instructional Strategies for Transition* by David W. Test.
(2012, Paul H. Brookes Publishing Co., Inc.)

Teaching procedures

Prior to the lesson
1. Pre-prepare cleaning supplies for students.

Instructional procedures
1. Teacher will demonstrate using a verbal plus model prompt of how to place the headphones on the head and how to operate the on/off switch of the cassette recorder.
2. Teacher will demonstrate steps of the task analysis one time after the headphones are put on.
3. Teacher will say, "Turn on and begin work" and will instruct student to push the on button and listen to the first step of the task analysis.
4. Teacher will instruct student on how to turn the cassette off when they hear a "beep" after the verbal prompt is announced on the cassette.
5. Student will then verbalize the task step and complete it.
6. Give student 5 seconds from the time they turn off the cassette to begin the step.
7. Student has to complete the step without stopping for longer than 5 seconds.
8. After completing the step, student will turn the cassette player on again.
9. Student will listen to the verbal description of the next step.
10. Student will turn off the cassette player after the beep.
11. Student will verbalize the step.
12. Student will complete the step.
13. This process will be completed for the remainder of the task analysis.
14. Teacher should provide verbal praise for correct responses.
15. Provide a least-to-most prompt system if student does not begin to perform the step correctly within 5 seconds or made any type of error: verbal prompt (e.g., wet cloth); verbal and model prompt (e.g., pick up broom)
16. Teacher will create additional tapes that have a sequence of steps of each task analysis omitted.
17. Teacher will then require student to verbalize omitted steps and complete them.
18. The first tape involves teacher omitting the verbal description of the last step of task analysis.
19. The next step involves the teacher omitting the verbal description of the last two steps of the task analysis.
20. This process is continued for the remaining tasks.
21. If student does not complete or say the omitted step(s), teacher will verbalize it and have the student repeat it.

Evaluation

Data should be collected on the percent correct of the steps completed independently on the three separate task analyses. Students should complete a skill with 100% for one session. Student will complete each additional tape at 100% for one day. Skill generalization should be measured using the same procedure.

Lesson plan based on
Mitchell, R.J., Schuster, J.W., Collins, B.C., & Gassaway, L.J. (2000). Teaching vocational skills with a faded auditory prompting system. *Education and Training in Mental Retardation, 35,* 415–427.

research-to-practice lesson plan for using response prompting to teach how to clean a bathroom mirror, sink, and toilet.

Response prompting relates to Indicator 13 because practitioners can use the strategy as a type of transition service to teach an employment skill. It also can be written in an IEP objective to support a student's postsecondary independent living goals based on assessment results. It also relates to the SCCI essential knowledge and skills. Using response prompting requires active listening and critical thinking skills to interpret the information presented in order to perform the desired behavior.

SUMMARY

Teaching employment skills has gained more attention in the literature because of the need to increase the employment rate of students with disabilities. Researchers have identified secondary-level evidence-based practices that are designed to increase the employment skills of students with disabilities. Therefore, it is imperative that these practices are made available to practitioners so they know how to implement the practices in the classroom and the community. The information presented in this chapter provides practitioners with information needed to use these practices to improve the employment skills of students with disabilities.

FOR FURTHER INFORMATION

What Can You Do? The Campaign for Disability Employment (http://www.whatcanyoudo campaign.org/)

Provides information to promote positive employment outcomes for people with disabilities by encouraging the public to recognize the talent people with disabilities have to offer businesses

Office of Disability Employment Policy (http://www.dol.gov/odep/pubs/fact/stats.htm)

Provides statistics on the employment rate of people with disabilities

Virginia Commonwealth University Rehabilitation Research and Training Center (http://www.worksupport.com/about_us/index.cfm)

Provides information on the supports that are effective for assisting people with disabilities in maintaining their employment and furthering their careers

7

Bound for Success: Teaching Life Skills

April L. Mustian and Sharon M. Richter

Life skills instruction is included in the student development category of the Taxonomy for Transition Programming (Kohler, 1996), which focuses on instructional practices that emphasize life, employment, and occupational skill development. Life skills instruction is a specific subcategory of student development that includes leisure and social skills training; self-determination skills training, including goal setting, decision making, and self-advocacy; independent living skills training; and learning strategy skills training.

WHAT ARE LIFE SKILLS?

Life skills, as the term implies, are essential to life for all people, including individuals with intellectual disabilities. If an individual cannot perform life skills, another person will have to perform these skills for the individual (Brolin, 1989). Unlike knowledge of art and chemistry, which are skills that are important to success in certain settings such as a museum or a high school classroom, life skills are unique in that these skills are important to everyday functioning in *all* of the settings of life—home, school, and the community. People perform life skills every day in order to fulfill the varied roles of adult life, such as purchasing clothing, cashing a check, buying food at the grocery store, attending a course at the community college, taking medication when needed, taking public transportation to get to school, and working. Given that these skills are often prerequisites to independence and personal safety, acquiring these skills is critical to quality of life for all individuals. Therefore, life skills instruction is essential.

Life skills are generally grouped into five broad clusters: self-care and domestic living; recreation and leisure; communication and social skills; vocational skills; and other skills vital for community participation, such as postsecondary education (Nietupski, Hamre-Nietupski, Curtin, & Shrikanth, 1997).

WHY IS LIFE SKILLS INSTRUCTION DIFFERENT?

Many life skills can be taught via traditional classroom instruction. In other words, many life skills can be taught in the same manner that one would teach students how to complete multiplication problems or decode new words. However, given that most life skills are learned so that students may participate more fully in their communities, teachers should also employ instructional strategies that are specifically designed to teach life skills to students with disabilities. To do so, special educators must design instruction for students with disabilities that considers the settings in which they are typically used. For example, if a student must learn to use a time clock at his or her job, the teacher should use the characteristics of the time clock and the room where it is located as a reference point to adequately prepare students to use the time clock at work. Similarly, if a student must learn to make purchases at a store, the teacher should consider the common characteristics of cash registers and cashiers when designing instruction. In both of these examples, teachers will likely provide some instruction in the community sites via community-based instruction, as discussed in Chapter 3.

IMPORTANCE OF LIFE SKILLS INSTRUCTION

Students with disabilities who exit high school with proficient life skills have better post-school outcomes than those students who do not. For example, Roessler, Brolin, and Johnson (1990) found students who had good daily living skills at high school exit were more likely to have a higher quality of life (i.e., independent living) and be engaged in post-school employment. In addition, Blackorby, Hancock, and Siegel (1993) found students with high self-care skills were more likely to be engaged in postsecondary education, employment, and independent living than those with low self-care skills. As a result, experts in the field have recommended students with disabilities receive explicit instruction and training in leisure skills, self-care, social skills, and other adaptive behavior skills.

Explicit life skills instruction is often characterized by breaking down complex tasks into smaller instructional units, step-by-step modeling and guided practice, a wide range of examples and nonexamples, immediate corrective feedback, and multiple opportunities to practice specific skills (Archer & Hughes, 2010).

EVIDENCE-BASED PRACTICES IN LIFE SKILLS INSTRUCTION

The National Secondary Transition Technical Assistance Center (NSTTAC) has identified 48 evidence-based practices that have been used to teach students with disabilities across a range of life skills and instructional approaches. Table 7.1 displays the list of all evidence-based practices identified for life skills development. Each practice includes the following:

1. The level of evidence (strong, moderate, potential) as defined by NSTTAC

2. With whom the practice has been implemented

3. How the skill or instruction has been implemented

4. The setting or settings in which the life skill has been implemented

5. How the skill relates to the items on the Indicator 13 checklist

6. How the skill relates to the common core standards

7. The best place to find out how to teach the skill, with links to sample lesson plan starters

8. References used to establish the evidence base

Table 7.1.   Evidence-based practices in life skills development

Instructional strategy	Skill
Using backward chaining to teach	Functional life skills
Using computer-assisted instruction to teach	Food preparation and cooking skills Functional life skills Grocery shopping skills
Using community-based instruction to teach	Communication skills Community integration skills Functional life skills Grocery shopping skills Purchasing skills
Using constant time delay to teach	Applied math skills Banking skills Communication skills Food preparation and cooking skills Functional life skills Leisure skills Purchasing skills
Using forward chaining to teach	Home maintenance skills
Using general case programming to teach	Safety skills
Using the one-more-than strategy to teach	Counting money Purchasing skills
Using progressive time delay to teach	Functional life skills Purchasing skills Safety skills
Using response prompting to teach	Food preparation and cooking skills Functional life skills Grocery shopping skills Home maintenance skills Laundry tasks Leisure skills Purchasing skills Safety skills Sight word reading Social skills
Using self-management instruction to teach	Social skills
Using self-monitoring to teach	Functional life skills
Using simulations to teach	Banking skills Functional life skills Purchasing skills Social skills
Using a system of least-to-most prompts to teach	Communication skills Food preparation and cooking skills Functional life skills Grocery shopping skills Purchasing skills Safety skills
Using a system of most-to-least prompts to teach	Functional life skills
Using total task chaining to teach	Functional life skills
Using video modeling to teach	Food preparation and cooking skills

Each practice description also provides links on NSTTAC's web site (http://www.nsttac.org) to research-to-practice lesson plan starters. The lesson plan starters are perhaps the most practical resource for classroom use. Each lesson plan starter contains a lesson objective, setting and materials, content taught, teaching procedures, evaluation method, and the research study on which the lesson plan was based. Several of these practices and accompanying lesson plan starters are described in more detail in the following sections.

Using the One-More-Than Strategy to Teach Purchasing Skills

Using the one-more-than strategy to teach purchasing skills has been identified as an evidence-based practice by the NSTTAC. It has been implemented with students with moderate intellectual disabilities and autism spectrum disorders, with ages ranging from 14 to 17 years. The one-more-than technique combined with cents-pile modification is a strategy to increase students' abilities to use money for purchases (Denny & Test, 1995). By using this functional strategy, learners can successfully purchase items by using currency without having to master skills related to coin usage and coin value, which can be barriers to successful purchasing in the community. Specifically, it can be used to teach individuals to pay one more dollar than requested (e.g., cost is $3.29 and the individual gives $4.00). The one-more-than strategy has been used to teach independent purchases (Cihak & Grim, 2008), making community purchases (Denny & Test, 1995), and purchasing grocery items (Ayres, Langone, Boon, & Norman, 2006). It has been implemented in both the school and community settings.

Figure 7.1 provides more complete information about using the one-more-than strategy to teach purchasing skills. The practice description for using the one-more-than strategy to teach purchasing skills provides two lesson plan starters (i.e., community purchases, independent purchases) for practitioners to use when implementing this evidence-based practice in the classroom. The lesson plan starter for using the one-more-than strategy to teach community purchases is displayed in Figure 7.2.

Using Constant Time Delay to Teach Banking Skills

Using constant time delay (CTD) to teach banking skills is another evidence-based practice identified by NSTTAC. It has been implemented with students with moderate intellectual disabilities, with ages ranging from 14 to 20 years. In CTD, several trials are first presented using a zero-second delay between the presentation of the natural stimulus and the response prompt. The trials that follow the simultaneous prompt condition apply a fixed time delay, such as 3 or 5 seconds (Cooper et al., 2007). In the studies used to establish the evidence base for using CTD to teach banking skills, CTD included using a 3-second constant time delay (McDonnell & Ferguson, 1989) and a 3-second time delay in combination with video modeling, community-based instruction (CBI), and simulation (Branham et al., 1999). The specific banking skills taught using CTD are cashing a check, writing a check, and using an automated teller machine (ATM). This practice has been implemented in a self-contained classroom and in the community setting.

Figure 7.3 provides more detailed information on using CTD to teach banking skills. In addition, see Chapter 3 for more information on using CTD. The practice description for using CTD to teach banking skills provides one research-to-practice lesson plan starter for practitioners to use in order to implement this evidence-based practice in the classroom. This lesson plan starter was created specifically for teaching students to cash checks and use an ATM (see Figure 7.4).

Using Response Prompting to Teach Sight Word Reading

Using response prompting to teach sight word reading is an evidence-based practice identified by NSTTAC. This practice has been implemented with students who have moderate and severe intellectual disabilities, with ages ranging from 14 to 26 years. Response prompting

Using One-More-Than Strategy to Teach Purchasing Skills

What is the evidence base?

A moderate level of evidence based on three moderate-quality single-subject studies

With whom was it implemented?

Students with
- Moderate intellectual disabilities (two studies, $n=7$)
- Autism (one study, $n=4$)

Ages ranging from 14 to 17
Males ($n=6$), females ($n=5$)
Ethnicity
- None reported ($n=11$)

What is the practice?

The one-more-than strategy is used to teach individuals to pay one more dollar than requested. (e.g., cost is $3.29 and the individual gives $4.00; Denny & Test, 1995). It is also referred to as "next dollar," "counting on," or "dollar more" strategy.

How has the practice been implemented?

One-more-than strategy has been used to teach
- Independent purchases (Cihak & Grim, 2008)
- Making community purchases (Denny & Test, 1995)
- Purchasing grocery items (Ayres, et al., 2006)

Where has it been implemented?

School and community (one study)
School (one study)

Where is the best place to find out how to do this practice?

The best place to find out how to implement *one-more-than strategy* is through the following research to practice lesson plan starters:

> - Using the one-more-than strategy to teach community purchases:
> http://www.nsttac.org/LessonPlanLibrary/46.pdf
> - Using the one-more-than strategy to teach independent purchases:
> http://www.nsttac.org/LessonPlanLibrary/LessonPlanCihakandGrim2008nextdollar.pdf

How does this practice relate to Indicator 13?

Indicator 13 checklist Item 3: Teaching purchasing skills may reflect results of transition assessment information.

Indicator 13 checklist Item 4: Purchasing skills may be a transition service designated in an IEP that will enable a student to meet his or her postsecondary independent living goal(s)

Indicator 13 checklist Item 6: Teaching purchasing skills may be an IEP objective that supports a student's postsecondary independent living goal(s)

How does this practice relate to common core standards?

Understand ratio concepts and use ratio reasoning to solve problems (Grade 6)
- Use ratio and rate reasoning to solve real-world and mathematical problems.

Comprehension and collaboration (Grade 8)
- Integrate and evaluate information presented in diverse media and formats, including visually, quantitatively, and orally.

Knowledge of language (Grade 8)
- Use knowledge of language and its conventions when writing, speaking, reading, or listening.

References used to establish this evidence base

Ayres, K.M., Langone, J., Boon, R.T., & Norman, A. (2006). Computer-based instruction for purchasing skills. *Education and Training in Developmental Disabilities, 41,* 252–263.
Cihak, D., & Grim, J. (2008). Teaching students with autism spectrum disorder and moderate intellectual disabilities to use counting-on strategies to enhance independent purchasing skills. *Research in Autism Spectrum Disorders, 1,* 716–727.
Denny, P.J., & Test, D.W. (1995). Using the one-more-than technique to teach money counting to individuals with moderate mental retardation: a systematic replication. *Education and Treatment of Children, 18,* 422–432.

Figure 7.1. Practice description for using the one-more-than strategy to teach purchasing skills. (From National Secondary Transition Technical Assistance Center. [2011]. *Using one-more-than strategy to teach purchasing skills.* Charlotte, NC: Author.)

Purchasing Items Using "One-More-Than" Technique

Objective: To teach purchasing skills by using the "one-more-than" technique with the "cents-pile modification" with 1-, 5-, and 10-dollar bills

Setting: Instruction is conducted in the school library four times each week. Skill generalization is measured in the community at stores and restaurants near the school.

Materials: Each student was given five 1-dollar bills, one 5-dollar bill, and one 10-dollar bill during all instructional sessions.

Content taught

The one-more-than technique with the cents-pile modification is a strategy to increase students' abilities to use money for purchases. By using this functional strategy, learners can successfully purchase items by using currency without mastery of skills related to coin usage and coin value, which can be barriers to successful purchasing in the community.

The following description of this strategy has been developed based on information in the article.

1. The purchaser listens for the price of an item (e.g., "Three dollars and forty-eight cents").

2. The purchaser counts one dollar for the "cents pile" (i.e., 48 cents) and puts it aside.

3. The purchaser then places the number of dollar bills identified in the price (i.e., three) and places these on the cents-pile dollar.

4. The purchaser then pays for the item using all of the bills in the pile.

Teaching procedures

1. Tell students that you will teach them a method they can use to go to the store and buy things themselves.

2. Orally describe and model to introduce the concept of one-more-than with cents-pile modifications. For example, say, "If the salesperson says, 'two dollars and fifteen cents,' you put one dollar to the side for the cents pile, and then count out two dollars."

3. Tell students they are going to role-play purchasing items using the method.

4. Separate training items into four price groups, 0–$4.99, $5.00–$9.99, $10.00–$14.99, and $15.00–$20.00.

Figure 7.2. Research-to-practice lesson plan starter for using one-more-than strategy to teach purchasing skills.

From National Secondary Transition Technical Assistance Center. (2008).
Purchasing items using "one-more-than" technique. Charlotte, NC: Author.

In *Evidence-Based Instructional Strategies for Transition* by David W. Test.
(2012, Paul H. Brookes Publishing Co., Inc.)

5. For the first price group, 0–$4.99, students will use the cents-pile modification to count out one more dollar than the amount requested.

6. Name a price between 0–$4.99 in one of the following ways:
   a. With the terms *dollars* and *cents* included (e.g., "That will be four dollars and twenty cents")
   b. Without dollars and cents (e.g., "That will be four twenty")

7. Model paying the first training amount by counting one dollar to the side for the cents pile and then count out the number of dollars requested.

8. Have students practice paying the first training amount.

9. For each correct response, provide descriptive verbal praise on a continuous schedule of reinforcement schedule by pointing out that the student had just given enough dollars to pay for items, such as "Good job. You just gave me enough dollars."

10. For each incorrect response, verbally describe and model the correct response and then have the student try again. If student then responds appropriately, provide praise. If the student responds incorrectly, move to the next item by saying, "Let's try another one."

11. Provide students with three additional training amounts from the same price group using one of the ways to state the price identified in Item 6 above.

12. Use the same procedure for all price groups with additional instruction related to counting on from 5- and 10-dollar bills.

13. Show the students the bill(s), model counting-on from the bill(s), and then model the example item for that price group (e.g., for 7 dollars, start with a 5-dollar bill and count on). As you place a 5-dollar bill on the table, say, "Five." As you place each dollar bill on the 5-dollar bill, say "six" as you place the first bill and "seven" as you place the next bill on the money stack.

14. Ask students to repeat the modeled item.

15. During training sessions, use 12 amounts that were not used in previous training sessions.

16. When students achieve 12 correct responses out of 12 opportunities, present mixed practice to students by randomly distributing three amounts from each of the four price groups across the 12 training items.

Evaluation

Collect student performance data on the percent correct on 12-item daily probes. Probes should include prices from the different price ranges and be stated to students in one of the following ways:

1. With the terms *dollars* and *cents* included (e.g., "That will be five dollars and twenty cents")

2. Without dollars and cents (e.g., "That will be five twenty")

Lesson plan based on
Denny, P., & Test, D. (1995). Using the one-more-than technique to teach money counting to individuals with moderate mental retardation: A systematic replication. *Education & Treatment of Children, 18,* 422–432.

From National Secondary Transition Technical Assistance Center. (2008).
Purchasing items using "one-more-than" technique. Charlotte, NC: Author.

In *Evidence-Based Instructional Strategies for Transition* by David W. Test.
(2012, Paul H. Brookes Publishing Co., Inc.)

Using Constant Time Delay to Teach Banking Skills

What is the evidence base?

A potential level of evidence based on two acceptable quality single-subject studies

With whom was it implemented?

Students with moderate intellectual disabilities (two studies, $n=7$)
Ages ranged from 14–20
Males ($n=2$), females ($n=1$)
• Gender not specified (one study, $n=4$)
Ethnicity
• None reported ($n=7$)

What is the practice?

Constant time delay (CTD) has been defined as first presenting several trials using a zero-second delay between the presentation of the natural stimulus and the response prompt. The trials that follow the simultaneous prompt condition apply a fixed time delay (e.g., 3 seconds or 5 seconds; Cooper, Heron, & Heward, 2007).

In the studies used to establish the evidence base for using CTD to teach banking skills, CTD included using a
• Three-second CTD in combination with video modeling, community-based instruction, and simulation (Branham,, Collins, Schuster, & Kleinert, 1999)
• Three-second CTD (McDonnell & Ferguson, 1989)

How has the practice been implemented?

CTD was used in combination with video modeling, community-based instruction, and simulation to teach
• Cashing a check (Branham et al., 1999)
CTD was used to teach
• Writing a check
• Using an ATM (McDonnell & Ferguson, 1989)

Where is the best place to find out how to do this practice?

The best place to find out how to implement CTD is through the following research to practice lesson plan starter:

> • Using CTD to teach banking
> http://www.nsttac.org/LessonPlanLibrary/LessonPlanMcDonnellFergusonbanking.pdf

Where has it been implemented?

Self-contained classroom and community (one study)
Community bank (one study)

How does this practice relate to Indicator 13?

Indicator 13 checklist Item 3: Teaching banking skills may reflect results of transition assessment information

Indicator 13 checklist Item 4: Conducting bank transactions may be a transition service designated in an individualized education program (IEP) that will enable a student to meet his or her postsecondary independent living goal(s)

Indicator 13 checklist Item 6: Teaching banking skills may be an IEP objective that supports a student's postsecondary independent living goal(s)

How does this practice relate to common core standards?

Understand ratio concepts and use ratio reasoning to solve problems (Grade 6)
• Use ratio and rate reasoning to solve real-world and mathematical problems, such as by reasoning about tables of equivalent ratios, tape diagrams, double number line diagrams, or equations.
Comprehension and collaboration (Grade 8)
• Integrate and evaluate information presented in diverse media and formats, including visually, quantitatively, and orally.
Knowledge of language (Grade 8)
• Use knowledge of language and its conventions when writing, speaking, reading, or listening.

References used to establish this evidence base

Branham, R.S., Collins, B.C., Schuster, J.W., & Kleinert, H. (1999). Teaching community skills to students with moderate disabilities: Comparing combined techniques of classroom simulation, videotape modeling, and community-based instruction. *Education and Training in Mental Retardation and Developmental Disabilities, 34,* 170–181.

McDonnell, J., & Ferguson, B. (1989). A comparison of time delay and decreasing prompt hierarchy strategies in teaching banking skills to students with moderate handicaps. *Journal of Applied Behavior Analysis, 22,* 85–91.

Figure 7.3. Practice description for using constant time delay to teach banking skills. (From National Secondary Transition Technical Assistance Center. [2011]. *Using constant time delay to teach banking skills.* Charlotte, NC: Author.)

Cashing Checks and Using an ATM

Objective: To teach students to make a cash withdrawal at an automated teller machine (ATM) or write checks for cash

Setting: Bank

Materials:
1. ATM card
2. Check writing materials: checks and withdrawal slips
3. Optional materials for students requiring additional supports:
   - A cue card that provides students with the correct spelling and format for the written dollar values to be entered on the check
   - A complete model of a check for cash in the amounts of $10 and $20

Content taught

Students are taught to withdraw money from a bank one of two ways. They are taught to withdraw $10 and $20 by accessing an ATM or by writing checks for cash at a bank.

Task analysis for use of the ATM
1. Insert the access card.
2. Enter the personal identification number.
3. Press the button indicating that the correct number has been entered.
4. Press the button to indicate a withdrawal from a checking account.
5. Enter 1000 or 2000 to indicate dollar and cent amount.
6. Press the *Correct* button.
7. Lift the door and remove the bill.
8. Press the button to indicate end of transaction.
9. Remove the access card and receipt from the appropriate slots.

Task analysis for writing a check
1. Enter the bank and move to a table.
2. Enter the correct date on the check.
3. Write the word *CASH* on the appropriate line.
4. Enter the appropriate dollar value (i.e., 10.00 or 20.00).
5. Write the dollar value on the correct line (i.e., *Ten and 00/100* or *Twenty and 00/100*).
6. Sign the check.

(continued)

Figure 7.4. Research-to-practice lesson plan starter for using constant time delay to teach banking skills.

From National Secondary Transition Technical Assistance Center. (2008). *Cashing checks and using an ATM.* Charlotte, NC: Author.

In *Evidence-Based Instructional Strategies for Transition* by David W. Test.
(2012, Paul H. Brookes Publishing Co., Inc.)

7. Cash the check.
8. Exit the bank.

Teaching procedures

Pretest procedures
1. Begin the session by providing the student with the necessary materials (e.g., access card, checkbook, pen) and a verbal prompt (e.g., "Withdraw ___ dollars from the money machine" or "Write and cash a check for ___dollars.").
2. Each student should withdraw $10 and $20 during each probe session.
3. If the student makes an error, except for signing their name, complete the step for them and prompt them to finish the activity.
4. If the student makes an error while signing their name, physically assist them in signing without providing additional feedback. Prompt the student to finish the rest of the task.
5. At the end of the session, return the money that was withdrawn into the appropriate account.
6. Collect data on the number of steps completed correctly.

Instructional procedures

1. Instructional sessions should last 20 minutes; students should receive two to six trials per session and at least one trial on each of the two target amounts (i.e., $10 and $20) during each instruction session.
2. Assistance during instruction should be provided using the prompt hierarchy and faded by reducing the level of prompting on the hierarchy.
3. Prompt hierarchy:
   a. Physical assistance plus direct verbal cue
   b. Point plus direct verbal cue or model plus direct verbal cue
   c. Direct verbal cue
   d. Gesture
4. The initial prompt provided to students should be determined during pretesting procedures.
5. Prompts should be faded after two consecutive correct trials.
6. If students make an error, they should be prompted through the task by being prompted with the correct level on the hierarchy.

Evaluation

Students should perform 100% of the task analysis steps correctly for two consecutive sessions. Record the errors of each step of the tasks analyses if the student makes step initiation errors, discrimination errors, and response errors. Step initiation errors should be recorded when the student does not complete the step within 5 seconds after the prompt is given. Discrimination errors are recorded when the student performs the step out of sequence or if they fail to respond correctly. Response errors are recorded when there is an incomplete response given or if the student performs the step too slowly.

Lesson plan based on
McDonnell, J.J., & Ferguson, B. (1989). A comparison of time delay and decreasing prompt hierarchy strategies in teaching banking skills to students with moderate handicaps. *Journal of Applied Behavior Analysis, 22,* 85–91.

has been defined as a stimuli that later functions as extra cues and reminders for desired behavior. This type of prompting can come in visual, auditory, textual, or symbolic forms (Cooper et al., 2007). In the two studies used to establish the evidence base for using response prompting to teach home maintenance skills, response prompting included video prompts paired with verbal prompts (Taylor, Collins, Schuster, & Kleinert, 2002) and static picture prompts (Gaule, Nietupski, & Certo, 1985). This practice has been used to teach laundry and grocery store sight words and has been implemented in the supermarket and community settings.

Figure 7.5 provides a practice description with more detailed information on using response prompting to teach sight word reading. The practice description for using response prompting to teach sight word reading provides one research-to-practice lesson plan starter for practitioners to use in order to implement this evidence-based practice in the classroom. This lesson plan starter was created specifically for teaching laundry skills to students (see Figure 7.6).

Using Community-Based Instruction to Teach Grocery Shopping Skills

Using CBI to teach grocery shopping skills is an evidence-based practice identified by NSTTAC. It is a practice that has been implemented with students who have mild, moderate, and severe intellectual disabilities, with ages ranging from 17 to 20 years. As described in Chapter 3, CBI is instruction that occurs in the community setting in which targeted functional skills would naturally occur (Brown et al., 1983). In the studies used to establish the evidence base for using CBI to teach grocery shopping skills, instruction included CBI immediately followed by simulated instruction (Bates et al., 2001) and classroom-based instruction followed by CBI (Gaule et al., 1985). In the study by Bates et al. (2001), results indicated that simulated instruction paired with CBI was more effective than using CBI alone to teach students grocery shopping skills.

Figure 7.7 provides a practice description with more detailed information on using CBI to teach grocery shopping skills. The practice description for using CBI to teach grocery shopping skills provides one research-to-practice lesson plan starter for practitioners to use in order to implement this evidence-based practice in the classroom. This lesson plan starter was created specifically for teaching students to purchasing skills in the grocery store setting (see Figure 7.8).

TYPES OF INSTRUCTION USED IN LIFE SKILLS DEVELOPMENT

Among the research studies used to establish the 48 evidence-based practices on life skills development, 16 different instructional approaches were used. Specifically, effective strategies for teaching life skills to students with disabilities include the following:

- Backward chaining
- Computer-assisted instruction
- Community-based instruction
- Constant time delay
- Forward chaining
- General case programming

Using Response Prompting to Teach Sight Word Reading

What is the evidence base?

A potential level of evidence based on two acceptable quality single-subject studies

With whom was it implemented?

Students with
- Moderate intellectual disabilities (two studies, $n=5$)
- Severe intellectual disabilities (one study, $n=2$)

Ages ranged from 14 to 26
Males ($n=1$ females) ($n=6$ males)
Ethnicity
- None reported ($n=7$)

What is the practice?

Response prompting has been defined as a stimuli that later functions as extra cues and reminders for desired behavior. Can be visual, auditory, textual, or symbolic (Cooper, Heron, & Heward, 2007).

In the studies used to establish the evidence base for using response prompting to teach home maintenance skills, response prompting included
- Video prompts paired with verbal prompts (Taylor, Collins, Schuster, & Kleinert, 2002)
- Static picture prompts (Gaule, Nietupski, & Certo, 1985)

How has the practice been implemented?

Visual and verbal prompting has been used to teach
- Laundry sight words (Taylor et al., 2002)

Static pictures have been used to teach
- Grocery store sight words (Gaule, Nietupski, & Certo, 1985)

Where has it been implemented?

Supermarket (one study)
Community (one study)
School (two studies)

Where is the best place to find out how to do this practice?

The best place to find out how to implement response prompting is through the following research-to-practice lesson plan starter:

- Using response prompting to teach laundry sight words
  http://www.nsttac.org/LessonPlanLibrary/56_85.pdf

How does this practice relate to Indicator 13?

Indicator 13 checklist Item 3: Teaching sight word reading may reflect results of transition assessment information.

Indicator 13 checklist Item 4: Sight word reading may be a transition service designated in an individualized education program (IEP) that will enable a student to meet his or her postsecondary independent living goal(s).

Indicator 13 checklist Item 6: Teaching sight word reading may be an IEP objective that supports a student's postsecondary independent living goal(s).

How does this practice relate to states' Career Clusters Initiative: Essential Knowledge and Skills?

ESS02.01 Select and employ appropriate reading and communication strategies to learn and use technical concepts and vocabulary in practice.
- Determine the most appropriate reading strategy for identifying the overarching purpose of text.

ESS02.01.02 Demonstrate the use of the concepts, strategies, and systems for obtaining and conveying ideas and information to enhance communication in the workplace.
- Employ verbal skills when obtaining and conveying information.

References used to establish this evidence base

Gaule, K., Nietupski, J., & Certo, N. (1985). Teaching supermarket shopping skills using an adaptive shopping list. *Education and Training of the Mentally Retarded, 20,* 53–59.

Taylor, P., Collins, B.C., Schuster, J.W., & Kleinert, H. (2002). Teaching laundry skills to high school students with disabilities: Generalization of targeted skills and nontargeted information. *Education and Training in Mental Retardation and Developmental Disabilities, 37,* 172–183.

Figure 7.5.   Practice description for using response prompting to teach sight word reading. (From National Secondary Transition Technical Assistance Center. [2011]. *Using response prompting to teach sight word reading.* Charlotte, NC: Author.)

Laundry Skills

Objective: To teach students laundry skills

Setting: Family living classroom

Materials:
1. Laundry basket filled with laundry
2. Liquid detergent
3. Fabric softener sheets
4. Eight functional words (e.g., temperature, detergent, cycle) printed on 5" × 7" cards displayed on washer or dryer or on the laundry products being used

Content taught

Task analysis steps for doing laundry:

1. Carry laundry basket with clothes to washer.

2. Open the washer lid.

3. Put clothes in the washer.

4. Twist the lid and remove it from the bottle of liquid detergent.

5. Pour the correct amount into a measuring cup.

6. Replace the cap on the bottle of liquid detergent.

7. Pour detergent from the measuring cup into the washer.

8. Close the washer lid.

9. Select the correct cycle.

10. Select the water temperature.

11. Select the load size.

12. Press the button to start the washer.

13. When the last cycle has finished remove clothes from the washer.

Figure 7.6. Research-to-practice lesson plan starter for using response prompting to teach sight word reading. *(continued)*

From National Secondary Transition Technical Assistance Center. (2008). *Laundry skills.* Charlotte, NC: Author.

In *Evidence-Based Instructional Strategies for Transition* by David W. Test.
(2012, Paul H. Brookes Publishing Co., Inc.)

14. Put clothes in the dryer.

15. Put fabric softener sheet in the dryer.

16. Close the dryer door.

17. Select the desired setting.

18. Press the button to start the dryer.

19. When the dryer stops remove clothes from the dryer.

20. Remove clothes from the dryer and put them into the laundry basket.

Teaching procedures

1. Present materials.

2. Deliver intentional cue (i.e., "Are you ready to wash and dry clothes?") and wait for affirmative response.

3. Deliver task direction (e.g., "[Name], wash and dry the clothes.") and wait 5 seconds for student to begin step and 15 seconds for student to complete step.

4. If student performs step correctly, provide verbal praise and wait 5 seconds for student to initiate next step.

5. If student performs step incorrectly, fails to initiate a response within 5 seconds, or fails to complete a step within 15 seconds, repeat the task direction using a verbal prompt (e.g., "After you put clothes in the washer, twist lid and remove it from the detergent.") and wait 5 seconds for student to begin step and 15 seconds for student to complete step.

6. If student performs step incorrectly following verbal prompt, model the correct response along with verbal prompt and wait 5 seconds for student to begin step and 15 seconds for student to complete step.

7. Proceed in this manner delivering praise for correct responses or delivering next level of prompt hierarchy until student completes each step of task analysis.

Evaluation

Evaluate the student's performance by collecting data on the percentage of steps correct on the task analyses.

Lesson plan based on

Taylor, P., Collins, B.C., Schuster, J.W., & Kleinert, H. (2002). Teaching laundry skills to high school students with disabilities: Generalization of targeted skills and nontargeted information. *Education and Training in Mental Retardation and Developmental Disabilities, 37,* 172–183.

Using Community-Based Instruction to Teach Grocery Shopping Skills

What is the evidence base?

A potential level of evidence based on one acceptable quality group study and two acceptable quality single-subject studies

With whom was it implemented?

Students with
- Mild intellectual disability (one study, $n=20$)
- Moderate intellectual disability (one study, $n=20$)
- Moderate to severe intellectual disability (two studies, $n=9$)

Ages ranged from 16 to 20, two studies; mean age of 17.2 years, one group study

Males ($n=33$), females ($n=16$)

Ethnicity
- None reported (three studies, $n=49$)

What is the practice?

Community-based instruction (CBI) is teaching functional skills that take place in the community where target skills would naturally occur (Brown et al., 1983).

In the studies used to establish the evidence base for using CBI to teach grocery shopping skills, CBI
- Immediately followed simulated instruction (Bates, Cuvo, Miner, & Korabek, 2001)
- Followed a phase of instruction in the classroom (Gaule, Nietupski, & Certo, 1985)
- Was the only setting for instruction (Ferguson & McDonnell, 1991).

How has the practice been implemented?

Simulated instruction paired with CBI was more effective and efficient than CBI alone to teach students tasks associated with purchasing items in a grocery store, using a 32-step task analysis, including picture lists (Bates et al., 1999).

Response prompts (static picture cues) were used to teach students to locate, obtain, and purchase items in the grocery store during the second and third phases of instruction, following a first phase of classroom instruction (Gaule et al., 1985).

Concurrent sequencing, presenting all steps without controlling order, was used to teach selecting grocery items from a list (Ferguson & McDonnell, 1991). All instruction occurred in the community in this study.

Where has it been implemented?

Grocery stores (three studies)

Where is the best place to find out how to do this practice?

- Using CBI to teach purchasing skills
  RtPLP Starter, CBI to teach grocery shopping, Gaule et al., 1985.

How does this practice relate to Indicator 13?

Indicator 13 checklist Item 3: Teaching grocery shopping skills in the community may reflect results of transition assessment information.

Indicator 13 checklist Item 4: CBI on grocery shopping may be a transition service designated in an IEP that will enable a student to meet his or her postsecondary independent living goal(s).

Indicator 13 checklist Item 6: Teaching grocery shopping skills using CBI may be an IEP objective that supports a student's postsecondary independent living goal(s)

How does this practice relate to common core standards?

Reason quantitatively and use units to solve problems. (Number and Quantity, Grades 9–12)
- Use units as a way to understand problems and to guide the solution of multistep problems; choose and interpret units consistently in formulas; choose and interpret the scale and the origin in graphs and data displays.

Solve real-life and mathematical problems using numerical and algebraic expressions and equations. (Expressions and Equations, Grade 6)
- Use variables to represent two quantities in a real-world problem that change in relationship to one another.

(continued)

Figure 7.7.   Practice description for using community-based instruction to teach grocery shopping skills. (From National Secondary Transition Technical Assistance Center. [2011]. *Using community-based instruction to teach grocery shopping skills.* Charlotte, NC: Author.)

Figure 7.7.   *(continued)*

How does this practice relate to States' Career Clusters Initiative: Essential Knowledge and Skills?

Demonstrate mathematics knowledge and skills required to pursue the full range of postsecondary education and career opportunities (Academic Foundations).
*   Identify whole numbers, decimals, and fractions.
*   Demonstrate the use of relational expressions such as: equal to, not equal, greater than, or less than.
*   Demonstrate knowledge of basic arithmetic operations such as addition, subtraction, multiplication, and division.

Select and employ appropriate reading and communication strategies to learn and use technical concepts and vocabulary in practice (Communications).
*   Determine the most appropriate reading strategy for identifying the overarching purpose of a text (i.e., skimming, reading for detail, reading for meaning, or critical analysis).

References used to establish this evidence base

Bates, P.E., Cuvo, T., Miner, C.A., & Korabek, C.A. (2001). Simulated and community-based instruction involving persons with mild and moderate mental retardation. *Research in Developmental Disabilities, 22,* 95–115.

Fergusen, R., & McDonnell, J. (1991). A comparison of serial and concurrent sequencing strategies in teaching generalized grocery item location to students with moderate handicaps. *Education and Training in Mental Retardation, 26,* 292–304.

Gaule, K., Nietupski, J., & Certo, N. (1985). Teaching supermarket shopping skills using an adaptive shopping list. *Education and Training of the Mentally Retarded, 20,* 53–59.

*   The one-more-than strategy
*   Progressive time delay
*   Response prompting
*   Self-management instruction
*   Self-monitoring
*   Simulations
*   Least-to-most prompts
*   Most-to-least prompts
*   Total task chaining
*   Video modeling

Table 7.2 provides definitions for each type of instructional approach that has been used to teach life skills development.

SUMMARY

As evidenced by the practice descriptions and research-to-practice lesson plan starters described in this chapter, multiple instructional approaches have been used and found effective for teaching life skills. When choosing how best to teach life skills to students with disabilities, there are important considerations to acknowledge. First, if students require instruction to increase the probability that they will experience postsecondary success in the area of independent living, then teaching functional life skills should become a part of their transition plan, with generalization of such skills being the primary goal.

It is also important to consider cost-efficiency and access to resources when planning instruction in life skills development. For instance, although CBI is an evidence-based practice and has been mentioned multiple times in this text, some teachers may not have

Grocery Shopping

Objective: To teach students to prepare a shopping list, locate and obtain items from the supermarket, and purchase obtained items

Setting: Self-contained high school classroom and community grocery store

Materials:

1. Pictorial meal preparation manual:
    -   The manual contains picture recipes and is used to generate shopping lists for supermarket items.
    -   The first page contains pictures of necessary food items, as well as utensils needed in preparing the meal.
    -   In order to simplify the development of the shopping list, the teacher circles all of the food items on the page so students do not have to discriminate between food and nonfood items.

2. Adaptive shopping list:
    -   An adaptive shopping aid is placed in a three-ring binder that can be opened and put in the seat section of a shopping cart.
    -   The shopping aid contains pictures of all of the items for each student's recipe.
    -   Adjacent to each picture is a square that denotes the approximate cost. Each square represents a 50-cent interval. Thus, a quart of milk that costs $1.49 has three squares.
    -   Another feature of the shopping aid is the money line on which students mark off the number of squares to determine approximate cost. Students count number of dollars available for shopping and use a marking pen to indicate available funds for shopping.

Content taught

1. Shopping list preparation
    a. Obtain the adaptive shopping list from its storage area.
    b. Check off each food item depicted in the recipe on the shopping list.
    c. Erase checks from pictures of grocery items on hand.
    d. Count the number of $1.00 bills available for shopping.
    e. Mark a line designating the number of dollars available on the money line found on the shopping aid.

2. Locating and obtaining items from the supermarket
    a. Enter the store.
    b. Obtain a cart.
    c. Place the open shopping aid in the seat of the cart.
    d. Obtain the needed supermarket items within 30 minutes.

Figure 7.8. Research-to-practice lesson plan starter for using community-based instruction to teach grocery shopping skills.   *(continued)*

From National Secondary Transition Technical Assistance Center. (2008). *Grocery shopping.* Charlotte, NC: Author.

In *Evidence-Based Instructional Strategies for Transition* by David W. Test.
(2012, Paul H. Brookes Publishing Co., Inc.)

    e.   Cross out each item depicted on the shopping aid as it is obtained.

    f.   Check off the appropriate number of squares for each item on the money line as the item is obtained.

3. Purchasing obtained items

    a.   Enter the checkout lane with the cart.

    b.   Give the appropriate number of dollars to the clerk.

    c.   Receive and put away any change.

    d.   Pick up the sack of items.

    e.   Exit the store.

Teaching procedures

1. Shopping list preparation

    a.   At the beginning of each instructional session the teacher demonstrates the steps in the task sequence.

    b.   Three to five individual instructional trials are given to the student with the number of trials given dependent on the available time.

    c.   Each trial consists of presentation cues and materials indicated on task analysis.

    d.   The student is allowed to perform the task steps until the sequence is completed correctly or until an error is made.

    e.   Verbal praise is used to reinforce correct performance.

    f.   Incorrect responses are followed by

        i.   Verbal prompt

        ii.   Teacher modeling correct response and required imitation by student

        iii.   Verbal cues to perform task step and physical guidance

        iv.   Following error correction student is allowed to proceed to next step

        v.   Once the percentage of correctly performed task steps on initial instructional trial reaches 50% on three consecutive days, teacher demonstration at the beginning of the session is discontinued.

2. Locating and obtaining items from the supermarket

    •   The reinforcement and correction procedures are identical to shopping list preparation with the exception that no teacher model is provided upon arrival at the supermarket.

3. Purchasing obtained items

    •   The reinforcement and correction procedures are identical to locating and obtaining items from the supermarket.

Evaluation

Evaluate the student's performance by collecting data on the percentage of steps correct on the task analyses.

Lesson plan based on

Gaule, K., Nietupski, J., & Certo, N. (1985). Teaching supermarket shopping skills using an adaptive shopping list. *Education and Training of the Mentally Retarded, 20,* 53–59.

From National Secondary Transition Technical Assistance Center. (2008). *Grocery shopping.* Charlotte, NC: Author.

In *Evidence-Based Instructional Strategies for Transition* by David W. Test.
(2012, Paul H. Brookes Publishing Co., Inc.)

Table 7.2. Instructional approaches used to teach life skills

Instructional strategy	Definition	Skills taught
Backward chaining	All behaviors identified in the task analysis are initially completed by the trainer, except for the final behavior in the chain. When the learner performs the final behavior in the sequence at the predetermined criterion level, reinforcement is delivered and the next-to-last behavior is introduced (Cooper et al., 2007).	Functional life skills
Computer-assisted instruction	The use of a computer and other associated technology with the intention of improving students' skills, knowledge, or academic performance (Okolo, Bahr, & Rieth, 1993)	Cooking skills Food preparation skills Functional life skills Grocery shopping skills
Community-based instruction	Instruction of functional skills that takes place in the community where target skills would naturally occur (Brown et al., 1983)	Communication skills Community integration skills Functional life skills Grocery shopping skills Purchasing skills
Constant time delay	First uses several trials using a zero-second delay (the stimulus presentation of the natural stimulus and the response prompt). The trials that follow the zero-second prompt condition apply a fixed time delay (e.g., 3 seconds or 5 seconds; Cooper et al., 2007).	Applied math skills Banking skills Communication skills Cooking skills Food preparation skills Functional life skills Leisure skills Purchasing skills
Forward chaining	Behaviors identified in a task analysis are taught in their naturally occurring order. Reinforcement is delivered when the predetermined criterion for the first behavior in the sequence is achieved then the next step in the task analysis is taught (Cooper et al., 2007)	Home maintenance skills
General case programming	A systematic method for selecting teaching examples that represent the full range of stimulus and response variations in the natural setting (Cooper et al., 2007)	Safety skills
One-more-than strategy	A specific strategy that teaches individuals to pay one more dollar than requested (Denny & Test, 1995)	Counting money skills Purchasing skills
Progressive time delay	A prompting strategy that begins with zero-second delay between the presentation of the natural stimulus and the response prompt and then gradually and systematically extend the time delay, often in 1-second intervals (Cooper et al., 2007)	Functional life skills Purchasing skills Safety skills
Response prompting	A stimuli that later functions as extra cues and reminders for desired behavior. Can be visual, auditory, textual, or symbolic (Cooper et al., 2007).	Cooking skills Food preparation skills Functional life skills Grocery shopping skills Home maintenance skills Laundry skills Leisure skills Purchasing skills Safety skills Social skills
Self-management instruction	A person using behavior change strategies in order to change their own subsequent behavior (Cooper et al., 2007)	Social skills
Self-monitoring	A procedure whereby a person observes his behavior systematically and records the occurrence or nonoccurrence of a target behavior (Cooper et al., 2007)	Functional life skills

(continued)

Table 7.2. *(continued)*

Instructional strategy	Definition	Skills taught
Simulation	Use of simulations in the classroom that approximate the natural stimulus conditions and response topographies associated with the performance of functional skills (Bates et al., 2001)	Banking skills Functional life skills Purchasing skills Social skills
System of least-to-most prompts	Method used to transfer stimulus control from response prompts to the natural stimulus whenever the participant does not respond to the natural stimulus or make an incorrect response. Least-to-most prompts begin with the participant having the opportunity to perform the response with the least amount of assistance on each trial. Greater degrees of assistance are provided with each successive trial without a correct response (Cooper et al., 2007).	Communication skills Cooking skills Food preparation skills Functional life skills Grocery shopping skills Purchasing skills Safety skills
System of most-to-least prompts	Method used to transfer stimulus control from response prompts to the natural stimulus whenever the participant does not respond to the natural stimulus or make an incorrect response. Most-to-least starts with physically guiding participant through the performance sequence, then gradually reducing the amount of physical assistance provided as training progresses from session to session (Cooper et al., 2007).	Functional life skills
Total task chaining	A variation of forward chaining in which the learner receives training on each step in the task analysis during each session (Cooper et al., 2007)	Functional life skills
Video modeling	A strategy used most often to teach social and functional skills in which the desired behavior is modeled and captured on video and the target student is then taught to demonstrate the modeled behavior. Video modeling can be used with peers as models or with the target students themselves as models.	Cooking skills Food preparation skills

frequent access or the financial means to implement such instruction on a regular and consistent basis. Therefore, teachers should explore all the potentially effective strategies for teaching life skills so that they may choose the best contextual fit for their students. See Chapter 3 for information on combining simulated instruction with CBI.

FOR FURTHER INFORMATION

Evidence-based practices in life skills instruction (http://www.nsttac.org/ebp/student_development.aspx)

This web site provides practice descriptions under the taxonomy category of student development.

Research-to-practice lesson plan library (http://www.nsttac.org/LessonPlanLibrary/EmploymentSkills.aspx)

This web site provides the research-to-practice lesson plan library for all the lesson plans developed by NSTTAC.

8

Strategies for Teaching Academic Skills

Allison Walker and Kelly Kelley

Although the ultimate goal for most high school students is to complete their studies and graduate with a high school diploma after 4 years, national trend data on high school student dropout and completion rates do not show this happening. Laird, Cataldi, Kewal-Ramani, and Chapman indicated that a negative trend has become evident in the staggering number of students dropping out of high school: "Approximately 4 of every 100 students who were enrolled in public or private high schools in October 2005 left school before October 2006 without completing a high school program" (2008, p. 4).

Similarly, Laird et al. reported that "approximately 3.3 million students age 16 through 24 years old were not enrolled in high school and did not earn a high school diploma" (2008, p. 6). When examining the graduation rates of students with disabilities, data from the National Longitudinal Transition Study-2 indicated only 72% of students with disabilities completed high school with a high school diploma or certificate of completion between 1987 and 2003. Of the students with disabilities who did not complete high school, 36% reported that they did not complete their studies because they did not like their school experience and 17% reported that they had poor relationships with their teachers and other students. Youth with disabilities who dropped out of secondary school also were significantly less likely to engage in postsecondary education, work, or training for work shortly after high school. According to Kohler and Field (2003), one way to combat these issues is to encourage student-focused planning, which ensures that the student's coursework is based on his or her interests, preferences, and needs.

Similar to Kohler and Field (2003), Bost and Riccomini (2006) have identified principles of effective instruction to prevent dropout rates and increase student engagement. According to Bost and Riccomini, these principles include the following:

- Active engagement
- Providing the experience of success, content coverage, and opportunity to learn
- Grouping for instruction
- Scaffolded instruction
- Addressing forms of knowledge
- Organizing and activating knowledge
- Teaching strategically

- Making instruction explicit
- Teaching sameness

Actively engaging students with disabilities in learning specific skills can involve providing explicit instruction that systematically presents content to learners and should also lead to opportunities to succeed so that they can have positive school experiences. The What Works in Transition Research Synthesis Project has built upon these principles identified by Bost and Riccomini (2006) by compiling a comprehensive list of evidence-based practices. Practitioners can use this list, which is available on the NSTTAC web site (http://www.nsttac.org/), to teach academic skills to high school students with disabilities. These practices include self-management, technology-based instruction, academic peer assistance, visual displays, and mnemonics.

All of the principles identified by Bost and Riccomini (2006) stress the importance of presenting information to students in an organized manner so that they can learn material and also achieve academic success.

Practitioners can help to increase student academic success by teaching sameness. Practitioners should design instruction across content areas to show common knowledge and teach students how to make connections.

SELF-MANAGEMENT

Self-management has been defined as "methods used by students to manage, monitor, record and/or assess their behavior or academic achievement" (Reid, Trout, & Schartz, 2005, p. 362). Because self-management has also been used as an umbrella term or synonym for self-monitoring, self-evaluation, self-instruction, goal setting, and strategy instruction, it is important to define each term to help understand the broader term of self-management and how it has been used to teach academic skills. See Table 8.1 for a list of self-management terms and corresponding definitions.

What Does Research Say About Self-Management and Academics?

Using self-management to teach academic skills to high school students with disabilities has been identified as an evidence-based practice by the What Works Transition Research Synthesis Project. In the 17 studies reviewed, five studies taught students to self-monitor, two stud-

Table 8.1. Terms and definitions of self-management

Term	Definition
Self-monitoring	Multistage process of observing and recording one's behavior
Self-evaluation	A process wherein a student compares his or her performance to a previously established criterion set by student or a teacher and is awarded reinforcement based on achieving the criterion
Self-instruction	Techniques that involve the use of self-statements to direct behavior
Goal setting	A process of a student self-selecting behavioral targets, which serve to structure student effort, provide information on progress, and motivate performance
Strategy instruction	Teaching students a series of steps to follow independently in solving a problem or achieving an outcome

Source: Mooney, Ryan, Uhing, Reid, and Epstein (2005).

ies taught students to self-evaluate, two taught students to self-instruct, one study taught students to set goals, one study taught students to use strategy instruction, and seven taught students to use a combination of these self-management components. The studies included 88 participants with learning disabilities, emotional/behavioral disorders, intellectual disabilities, attention-deficit/hyperactivity disorders, and severe disabilities.

How Has Self-Management Been Used to Teach Academic Skills?

Self-management has been used to teach academics in a variety of settings, including public secondary schools such as self-contained classrooms, private schools, and a summer school program. All studies included in the meta-analysis had positive results for using self-management to individuals with disabilities. For example, Carr and Punzo (1993) taught three males with emotional and behavioral disorders how to self-monitor academic accuracy and productivity in reading, mathematics, and spelling. Figure 8.1 is the research-to-practice lesson plan starter for this study.

In addition, DiGangi and Maag (1992) conducted a study in which students were taught to self-monitor, self-evaluate, and self-instruct between appropriate and inappropriate verbalizations using tally marks and evaluation questions. Results indicated students can be taught how to self-monitor and evaluate when explicitly taught. See Figure 8.2 for the research-to-practice lesson plan starter.

TECHNOLOGY-BASED INSTRUCTION

With many advances in technology, it has become a promising instructional strategy for teaching academic skills. First, to avoid confusion, it is important to define common terms associated with technology-based instruction:

- *Computer-based instruction* is simply when computers or associated technology are used to improve students' skills, knowledge, or academic performance (Okolo, Bahr, & Rieth, 1993).
- *Computer-assisted instruction* (CAI) includes software designed to provide instruction and practice for meeting specific learning objectives or goals with drill-and-practice or tutorial instruction (Kulik & Kulik, 1987; Posgrow, 1990).
- *Computer-enriched instruction* is the utilization of computer technology to augment instruction; it includes usage of the computer as a calculating tool, programming tool, and simulator (Kulik & Kulik, 1987).
- *Computer-managed instruction,* also called *integrated learning systems,* is the application of computer technology and extensive software programs designed to present sequential instruction to students over extended time periods while maintaining records of student progress (Kulik, 2003).

Combinations of technology-based interventions have been used effectively in research and classrooms to teach academic skills to students with disabilities.

What Does Research Say About
Technology-Based Instruction and Academics?

Technology-based instruction has been identified as an evidence-based practice by the What Works in Transition Research Synthesis Project to teach academic skills to students with

Using Self-Management to Improve Academic Accuracy and Productivity Performance

Objective: To teach students self-monitoring strategies/behaviors to improve academic accuracy and productivity performance

Setting: Classroom

Materials: Work tasks such as worksheets, a pencil, and self-recording sheets

Content taught

Students will learn self-monitoring skills to improve academic accuracy (number of items completed correctly), academic productivity (number of items completed daily), and on-task behavior (being seated, writing or calculating answers, or asking questions about tasks).

Teaching procedures

1. Provide students with an explicit definition of academic achievement using examples from student's previous work.
2. Discuss the importance of improving accuracy and productivity.
3. Instruct students to count the number of items given, number of items completed, and number of items answered correctly. Have the students write these numbers on a self-recording sheet and include available test scores (e.g., for spelling, students would count number of practices completed and number of words written correctly).
4. Model the self-monitoring procedure for students.
5. Ask students to repeat the definition of academic achievement and explain why it is important to monitor accuracy and productivity as well as demonstrate self-recording.
6. Once you provide explanations, have students begin self-monitoring and continue to correct and return student work at the end of each session without giving verbal feedback.
7. Continue giving students opportunities to self-monitor across other subject areas.

Evaluation

Collect data on academic accuracy, academic productivity, and on-task behavior by making anecdotal notes and/or collecting self-monitoring data sheets for each student.

Lesson plan based on

Carr, S.C., & Punzo, R.P. (1993). The effects of self-monitoring of academic accuracy and productivity on the performance of students with behavioral disorders. *Behavior Disorders, 18,* 241–250.

Figure 8.1.   Research-to-practice lesson plan starter for using self-management to improve academic accuracy and productivity performance.

From National Secondary Transition Technical Assistance Center. (2008).
Using self-management to improve academic accuracy and productivity performance. Charlotte, NC: Author.

In *Evidence-Based Instructional Strategies for Transition* by David W. Test.
(2012, Paul H. Brookes Publishing Co., Inc.)

Using Self-Management to Increase Appropriate Verbalizations

Objective: To teach students to self-monitor, self-evaluate/self-reinforce, and self-instruct to increase appropriate verbalization

Setting: Special education resource room

Materials: 3" × 5" index cards, a pencil, prompt card

Content taught

Students will be taught the difference between appropriate verbalizations and inappropriate verbalizations. Appropriate verbalizations are defined as "any utterance related to the assigned task such as asking for clarification, providing a positive acknowledgement for assistance received, demonstrating how to compute problems, or asking questions." Inappropriate verbalizations are defined as "interrupting a peer or teacher when talking to other students, making animal noises or grunts, yelling, swearing, or whistling in class."

Teaching procedures

1. First, teach students to self-monitor by making a tally mark on the left side of a 3" × 5" index card each time they have an appropriate verbal interaction or make an appropriate verbal statement. Have the students make a tally mark on the right side of the 3" × 5" index card each time they have an inappropriate verbal interaction or make an inappropriate verbal statement. Model and practice recording using appropriate and inappropriate verbal verbalizations.

2. For self-monitoring and self-evaluation/self-reinforcement, have the students glance at the tally card each time they mark it and ask themselves, "How is this working out? How am I doing?" (Be sure to include these questions on the index card and post on the student's desk as a reminder.) If the students feel they are doing well and have more tally marks on the appropriate side of their cards have them tell themselves, "I'm doing a great job."

Figure 8.2. Research-to-practice lesson plan starter for using self-management to increase appropriate verbalizations. *(continued)*

From National Secondary Transition Technical Assistance Center. (2008).
Using self-management to increase appropriate verbalizations. Charlotte, NC: Author.

In *Evidence-Based Instructional Strategies for Transition* by David W. Test.
(2012, Paul H. Brookes Publishing Co., Inc.)

3. For self-evaluation/self-reinforcement, students will no longer tally, but will continue asking, "How is this working out? How am I doing?" based on the index card on their desk. If they continue to do well, have them tell themselves, "I'm doing a great job."

4. For self-instruction, have the student learn how to ask for help by saying, "Do I understand what I'm working on?" "What don't I understand?" "How could I phrase it as a question?" "Would it be appropriate to ask a neighbor for help?" "Should I raise my hand or talk out loud?"

5. For self-instruction and self-monitoring, follow Step 1 above, but take away the self-monitoring tally cards and self-evaluative prompts.

For self-instruction, self-monitoring, and self-evaluation/self-reinforcement, use all three strategies as listed above and add self-reinforcement procedures described in Steps 2 and 3.

6. Finally, for self-instruction, self-evaluation/self-reinforcement, remove tally cards and replace cards that had self-evaluation prompts printed on them. Continue with self-instruction as described in Step 4.

Evaluation

Count appropriate and inappropriate verbalizations during a 15-minute seatwork period.

Lesson plan based on

DiGangi, S.A., & Maag, J.W. (1992). A component analysis of self-management training with behaviorally disordered youth. *Behavioral Disorders, 17,* 281–290.

From National Secondary Transition Technical Assistance Center. (2008).
Using self-management to increase appropriate verbalizations. Charlotte, NC: Author.

In *Evidence-Based Instructional Strategies for Transition* by David W. Test.
(2012, Paul H. Brookes Publishing Co., Inc.)

disabilities. A review of the literature found that technology-based instruction has been used to teach students reading, mathematics, writing, health topics, and other topics related to academic engagement and emotional recognition. The studies included a total of 1,491 participants with learning disabilities, traumatic brain injuries, Down syndrome, and intellectual disabilities.

How Has Technology Been Used to Teach Academic Skills?

Technology has been used to teach academics in a variety of settings including high school and middle school special education classrooms, as well as special schools such as private or residential settings. At least seven studies included in the meta-analysis did not report where the interventions had been implemented. All studies had positive results for using technology to individuals with disabilities.

Unfortunately, because of the specific software and technology used, it is hard for teachers to replicate how some of the interventions have been used in the studies. For example, many studies used specific programs that have been modified or are no longer available, such as Literacy and Technology Hands On (Gallaher, van Kraayenoord, Jobling, & Moni, 2002), Computer-based Informal Reading Inventory System (Bahr, Kinzer, & Rieth, 1991), Guide Hypermedia (Higgins, Boone, & Lovitt, 1996), Goods World Atlas (Horton & Lovitt, 1988), Student Assistant for Learning from Text (MacArthur & Haynes, 1995), the Grammar Examiner (Malouf, Wizer, Pilato, & Grogan, 1990), Drill multiplication practice program (Okolo, 1992), and MICROS observation system for measuring behavior (Rieth, Bahr, Okolo, Polsgrove, & Eckert, 1988).

ACADEMIC PEER ASSISTANCE

Peer assistance includes several strategies such as peer tutoring, cooperative learning, and peer instruction. Peer tutoring is simply the delivery of academic instruction by another student, either older or the same age as the tutee (Scruggs, Mastropieri, & Richter, 1985). Cooperative learning is when groups of students of different ability, sex, or ethnicity work together to achieve mutual goals (Tateyama-Sniezek, 1990). Peer instruction is when students are given specific roles to assist other students in completing an activity or teaching of a lesson (Hughes, Carter, Hughes, Bradford, & Copeland, 2002). Peer assistance has been used in a variety of ways to teach academics as well as social skill instruction.

What Does Research Say About Peer Assistance and Academics?

Using peer assistance to teach academic skills to high school students with disabilities has been identified as an evidence-based practice by the What Works in Transition Research Synthesis Project. In the 14 studies reviewed to identify peer assistance as an evidence-based practice, many studies used combinations of classroom peer tutoring, peer assistance, cooperative learning activities, student- and teacher-led instruction, and CAI. The studies included 165 participants with learning disabilities, emotional/behavioral disorders, moderate to severe disabilities, Down syndrome, and hearing impairments.

How Has Peer Assistance Been Used to Teach Academic Skills?

Peer assistance has been used to teach academics in a variety of settings, including public secondary schools, self-contained classrooms, and community settings. Peer assistance has been implemented with many age groups and disabilities, as well as in a variety of ways across academic subject areas. For example, Bahr and Rieth (1991) had students with disabilities work together to complete computer-assisted mathematics lessons and record their scores on the computer. Bell and Young (1990) and McDonnell, Mathot-Buckner, Thorson, and Fister (2001) used a classwide peer tutoring approach with teacher assigned tutor/learner dyads. Hawkins (1988) and Hawkins and Brady (1994) used student-directed instructional procedures during pauses from teacher-delivered lectures.

Undergraduate college students tutored students with learning disabilities in mathematics using four instructional phases including student approach assessments, coconstruction of new approaches, teaching of new approaches, and application of new approaches (Hock, Pulvers, Deschler, & Schumaker, 2001). In addition, Hughes et al. (2002) used conversational partners in instructional roles to assist with classroom assignments. See Figure 8.3 for the research-to-practice lesson plan starter for incorporating peers into noninstructional activities to facilitate social interaction.

Cooperative learning strategies have been used where peers serve as instructional supports to complete academics tasks (Miller, 1995; Wolford, Heward, & Alber, 2001; Wong, Butler, Ficzere, & Kuperis, 1997). Peer assistance has been used for completing, grading, and making corrections to homework assignments using cooperative homework team approaches (O'Melia & Rosenberg, 1994). Finally, individual peer tutoring approaches have been used with students without disabilities who were trained to assist students with disabilities in academic tasks (Martella, Marchand-Martella, Young, & MacFarlane, 1995; Schloss, Kobza, & Alper, 1997; Staub, Spaulding, Peck, Gallucci, & Schwartz, 1996). For example, in Schloss et al. (1997), peer tutoring was used to teach functional math skills (i.e., the next-dollar strategy) to adolescents with moderate intellectual disabilities (see Figure 8.4).

VISUAL DISPLAYS

Visual displays have been referred to in education by many different names, including graphic organizers, cognitive organizers, cognitive maps, structured overviews, tree diagrams, concept maps, and thinking maps (Boyle, 2000; Horton, Lovitt, & Bergerud, 1990; Hyerle, 1996, 2000). These visual displays have been used to help students organize complex ideas into meaningful topics within content areas and across disciplines (Hyerle, 1996). These displays can be used to help students describe characteristics of topics, understand the relationship between ideas, and the differences between ideas. Most important, visual displays are useful strategies that can be used at the elementary, middle, high school, and college levels.

What Does Research Say About Visual Displays?

Visual displays have been identified by the What Works in Transition Research Synthesis Project as an evidence-based practice to teach academic skills to high school students with disabilities. The studies included in the review to identify visual displays as an evidence-based practice included a total of 318 participants with learning disabilities. Two studies included

Using Noninstructional Activities to Increase Social Interactions

Objective: To set the occasion for students with and without disabilities to interact with each other during noninstructional activities

Setting: Classroom during academic class periods

Materials:

1. Leisure materials such as board games, magazines, art supplies
2. Television set
3. Desks or tables

Content taught

During noninstructional activities partners and participants were asked to engage in an activity that participants could perform without assistance. Activities varied across sessions and were selected from each participant's noninstructional activity pool. This pool contained only activities that were 1) consistent with participant's social or leisure IEP goals, 2) preferred by participants engaging in activities during "free time" periods, 3) activities participant could engage in without assistance, and 4) activities with duration of 10 minutes or more.

Teaching procedures

1. Give a directive statement to conversational partner and participant: "[Names of partner and participant], you two can do [name of activity] together" (e.g., "Natalie and Stacy, you two can read magazines together"). Chosen activities should relate to the participant's social or leisure IEP goals.
2. Provide assistance as needed to help partner and participant get needed materials or relocate to a different working area of room.
3. Begin observing partner and participant for 10 minutes after giving verbal instructions and when partners are within 5 feet of each other working.

Evaluation

Observe students and record occurrences of initiations and responses (both social- and activity-related) by participant and conversational partner. Score behaviors as "occurred" or "did not occur" at each 10-second interval for up to 10 minutes.

Lesson plan based on
Hughes, C., Carter, E.W., Hughes, T., Bradford, E., & Copeland, S.R. (2002). Effects of instructional versus noninstructional roles on the social interactions of high school students. *Education and Training in Mental Retardation and Developmental Disabilities, 37,* 146–162.

Figure 8.3. Research-to-practice lesson plan starter for using noninstructional activities to increase social interactions. (*Key:* IEP, individualized education program.)

From National Secondary Transition Technical Assistance Center. (2008).
Using noninstructional activities to increase social interactions. Charlotte, NC: Author.

In *Evidence-Based Instructional Strategies for Transition* by David W. Test.
(2012, Paul H. Brookes Publishing Co., Inc.)

Using Peer Tutoring to Teach the Next-Dollar Strategy

Objective: To teach money skills using the next-dollar strategy and reciprocal peer tutoring

Setting: Public classroom (simulated setting for acquisition), community settings (for generalization)

Materials:

1. Set of 24 payment amount index cards (3" × 5") prepared for student assessment (e.g., each contains a single printed dollar, decimal, and cent value; six cards each between $.39 and $.99, $1.25 and $1.99, $2.05 and $2.99, $3.15 and $3.99)

2. Additional set of fifteen 9" × 11" cards for peer tutors with the front and back of the card containing the same dollar amount as the assessment cards; on the side of the card facing the peer tutor include the dollar amount and a pictorial representation of the next higher dollar value (e.g., a pictorial display of two dollars could be printed under the dollar value $1.24 with the lower margin of the card containing a series of 15 boxes for the peer tutor to use to check if correct or incorrect responses are given)

3. Dollar bills (four $1 per dyad)

Content taught

Task analysis for using peer tutoring to teach the next-dollar strategy

1. Raise card

2. Wait for money (5 seconds)

3. Show reverse

4. Match money

5. Feedback: "That's right" or "That's wrong."

6. Score

7. If no answer, repeat Steps 1–6. If a match, put at the bottom of the pile and go to the next card.

Teaching procedures

Within the classroom (simulated)

1. For the first time the cards are used, teacher models using the cards by showing students the roles of the tutor and student following the task analysis described above.

2. Put the students in dyad groups and allow them to decide who will be the tutor and who will be the student.

Figure 8.4. Research-to-practice lesson plan starter for using peer tutoring to teach the next-dollar strategy.

From National Secondary Transition Technical Assistance Center. (2008).
Using peer tutoring to teach the next-dollar strategy. Charlotte, NC: Author.

In *Evidence-Based Instructional Strategies for Transition* by David W. Test.
(2012, Paul H. Brookes Publishing Co., Inc.)

3. Give the tutor the set of 15 cards in the one-dollar range and have them show the student side of the index card to the student. Instruct the tutor to ask the student how much would be needed to pay the amount shown and wait up to 5 seconds for the money to be placed on the desk.

4. Once the money is placed on the desk, have the tutor show the student the reverse side of the index card. The student should then match the dollar(s) that have been laid on the table to the dollars showing on the reverse side of the index card.

5. The tutor should use the task analysis steps to provide feedback such as "That's correct," "Good job," or "That's wrong."

6. If the student gets the answer correct, have the tutor record a plus in the scoring box on the back of the index card and return the card to the completed card pile.

7. If the student gets the answer incorrect after a 5-second wait time, have the tutor record a minus sign in the scoring box and repeat the procedure for that index card.

8. Cards that are scored as correct or incorrect are then returned to the pile for a second trial.

9. When all cards have been shown, have the dyad group switch roles and continue to reverse roles throughout a 15-minute instructional period.

10. Have the students exchange cards after every fourth session (e.g., one dollar, two dollars, three dollars, four dollars), but leave two or three of the cards from each of the previous training phases in the training card set.

Within the community (generalization)

11. At the end of the simulated classroom training, have the students practice the next dollar strategy at various fast food restaurants, stores, and recreation centers in the community.

12. Deliver an attentional cue such as, "Show how much you should pay for this?"

13. Allow the students to practice this in three to five community sites for 3 days and document their progress.

Evaluation

Student progress should be documented daily and recorded for each dyad based on percent answered correctly for each pair (e.g., six opportunities per participant for a correct response in each dollar phase). Students can move to next dollar amount (e.g., from $1.00 to $2.00) when each dyad has a combined total of 10–12 correct responses in each dollar amount being trained, as well as prior training amounts for two or more consecutive days.

Lesson plan based on

Schloss, P.J., Kobza, S.A., & Alper, S. (1997). The use of peer tutoring for the acquisition of functional math skills among students with moderate retardation. *Education and Treatment of Children, 20,* 189–208.

From National Secondary Transition Technical Assistance Center. (2008).
Using peer tutoring to teach the next-dollar strategy. Charlotte, NC: Author.

In *Evidence-Based Instructional Strategies for Transition* by David W. Test.
(2012, Paul H. Brookes Publishing Co., Inc.)

students who were considered prelingually deaf and two studies included students who were coded as having mental retardation. The 318 participants ranged from 13 to 16 years of age, with 15 being the average age; students were in Grades 6–10 for six of the studies. In addition, five studies included samples that were predominately male and one study included a sample of equally represented gender.

How Have Visual Displays Been Used to Teach Academic Skills?

According to the studies, visual displays have been used in the general education classroom at the middle school and high school levels and in the special education classroom in a resource and self-contained setting. Each of the 10 studies that used visual displays also included text with the displays to facilitate student learning. Examples of the following types of visual displays used across these studies included a tree diagram (Hollingsworth & Woodward, 1993), a Venn diagram (Boyle, 2000), an Euler diagram (Grossen & Carnine, 1990), and a picture of the water cycle (Diebold & Waldron, 1988). Of the 10 studies, five used visual displays to teach reading comprehension, three used the displays to teach concept instruction, two taught problem solving, and two used the displays as a fill-in organizer to help students learn information presented in an expository text. In addition, three studies had students developing the visual displays and writing the content, five studies included displays that were already developed and the student and/or teacher had to fill in the information, and two studies provided a whole visual display of the content information.

Not only was the type of content and type of display analyzed across the studies, but when the displays were used within the lesson was also examined. In other words, researchers found that eight studies used the displays after the material was presented to students, whereas two studies used the visual displays during the lesson. Also, researchers found that the duration of use of these displays ranged from one session to the displays being used across a semester. Last, the intensity of use of the displays ranged from 13 minutes to 1 hour, with an average intensity of 47.5 minutes.

MNEMONICS

Mnemonics include strategies such as memory-associate techniques, keyword mnemonics, and reconstructive elaborations, which are all used for the purpose of helping students memorize concepts by using keyword cues to facilitate learning. According to Mastropieri and Scruggs (1998), mnemonics have been known to be an effective form of instruction used with students with disabilities and an effective strategy for use on standardized and classroom tests.

Mnemonics can be used in language arts (i.e., vocabulary, spelling, and letter recognition), mathematics, science, social studies, foreign language, and other academic subjects (The Access Center, 2004).

What Does Research Say About Mnemonics?

Using mnemonics to teach academic skills to high school students with disabilities has been identified as an evidence-based practice by the What Works in Transition Research Synthesis Project. In the studies reviewed, a total of 669 participants were included with learning disabilities, emotional/behavioral disorders, and mental retardation. Participants' ages ranged from 13 to 17 years of age, with an average of 14 years of age. The grade level range reported across four studies was Grades 6–12.

How Have Mnemonics Been Used to Teach Academic Skills?

In 20 studies, mnemonics were used in special education classrooms, including resource and self-contained settings, general education classrooms including history and science classes, and small rooms available within schools. Three types of mnemonics were used across the 20 studies: keyword, keyword-pegword, and reconstructive elaborations. According to Wolgemuth, Cobb, and Alwell (2008), the keyword strategy uses visual and auditory cues to help students facilitate learning, whereas the keyword–pegword strategy is used with numbered or ordered information to help facilitate learning. Reconstructive elaborations were used in three studies by combining keywords and pictures to help students learn abstract information.

In 14 studies, the mnemonic intervention was administered by an experimenter; however, four studies had experimenters and/or teachers administer the intervention and two studies had experimenters teach the mnemonic strategy to small groups of students. Wolgemuth et al. found that the implementation of the mnemonic intervention ranged from one session to daily sessions over 8 weeks. In addition, the intensity of the intervention ranged from 9 minutes to a total of 34 hours.

HOW CAN TEACHERS USE THESE INTERVENTIONS WITHIN ONE LESSON?

Although educational practices such as visual displays and mnemonics have been identified individually as evidence-based practices, practitioners may not only use these practices individually but also may use a combination of these practices in a lesson. In Figure 8.5, a lesson plan has been developed to show how each practice (i.e., visual displays, mnemonics, technology, self-management, and academic peer assistance) can be used to teach a mathematical skill. For example, using the computer (i.e., technology) to show the symbol for each operation in conjunction with the mnemonic *Please Excuse My Dear Aunt Sally* and a visual display of the list of operations can help students learn the order of operations when completing a mathematical operation. The skill taught in this lesson can also be emphasized by having students use a graphic organizer as a form of strategy instruction (i.e., self-management), as well as partnering students with one another (i.e., peer assistance) to help solve each problem using the strategies provided in the lesson. Again, the use of these evidence-based strategies will not only have a positive impact on a student's acquisition of learning but can also provide opportunities for the student to be actively engaged in learning, which can ultimately lead to a student's success in graduating from high school.

FOR FURTHER INFORMATION

Dropout Prevention

National Dropout Prevention Center/Network (http://www.dropoutprevention.org)

Provides information on various resources and strategies to increase the graduation rate in America's schools

Peer Tutoring

Special Connections (http://www.specialconnections.ku.edu/cgi- bin/cgiwrap/specconn/main
.php?cat=instruction&section=cwpt/main)
Provides detailed information about classwide peer tutoring (CWPT) and how it can be
used in the classroom

Graphic Organizers

Teachnology (http://www.teach-nology.com/worksheets/graphic/)
Provides descriptions and visual examples of different types of graphic organizers

---

Content: Math

Grade level: Middle school

Objective: To teach students the correct order of operations in a mathematical equation.

Materials: Computer, worksheet, pen

Teaching procedures

1. Provide students with a written list of operations (e.g., parenthesis, exponents, multiplication, division, addition, and subtraction).

2. Show students a picture of each operation on the computer keyboard. For example, show the sign for addition (i.e., +).

3. Instruct each student to point to the sign on the keyboard and type the sign on the computer screen.

4. Point to the mnemonic on the board (i.e., **P**lease **E**xcuse **M**y **D**ear **A**unt **S**ally).

5. Instruct students that they must perform the operation in the parenthesis first, exponents second, multiplication third, division fourth, and subtraction fifth.

6. Instruct students to use the graphic organizer provided to them to fill in the correct order of each step of the mnemonic.

7. Show students a math problem on the board using numbers and mathematical operations.

8. Model how to solve the problem using the mnemonic.

9. Instruct students to solve three problems independently.

10. Instruct students to choose a partner and verbally describe to his/her partner how they used the mnemonic to solve the problem.

11. Instruct students to count the number of problems they solved correctly and the number of problems solved incorrectly.

12. If a student solved a problem(s) incorrectly, instruct the student's peer to help correct the problems using the mnemonic and/or graphic organizer.

Evaluation

Collect data on the accuracy of the order of operations used to solve each problem.

Figure 8.5. An example of using multiple interventions in a lesson.

References

Access Center. (2004). *Using mnemonic instruction to facilitate access to the general education curriculum.* Retrieved April 4, 2011, from http://www.k8accesscenter.org/training_resources/Mnemonics.asp

Agran, M., Blanchard, C., & Wehmeyer, M.L. (2000). Promoting transition goals and self-determination through student self-directed learning: The self-determined learning model of instruction. *Education and Training in Mental Retardation and Developmental Disabilities, 35,* 351–364.

Alberto, P.A., Cihak, D.F., & Gama, R.I. (2005). Use of static picture prompts versus video modeling during simulation instruction. *Research in Developmental Disabilities, 26,* 327–339.

Alberto, P.A., Taber, T.A., & Fredrick, L.D. (1999). Use of self-operated auditory prompts to decrease aberrant behaviors in students with moderate mental retardation. *Research in Developmental Disabilities, 20,* 429–439.

Alberto, P.A., & Troutman, A.C. (2009). *Applied behavior analysis for teachers* (8th ed.). Upper Saddle River, NJ: Pearson Education.

Allen, S., Smith, A., Test, D., Flowers, C., & Wood, W. (2002). The effects of self-directed IEP on student participation in IEP meetings. *Career Development for Exceptional Individuals, 24,* 107–120.

Ansell, D., & Casey Family Programs. (2009). *Ansell-Casey Life Skills Assessment (ACLSA).* Retrieved April 4, 2011, from http://www.caseylifeskills.org/pages/assess/assess_aclsa.htm

Archer, A.L., & Hughes, C.A. (2010). *Explicit instruction: Effective and efficient teaching.* New York: Guilford Press.

Ayres, K.M., Langone, J., Boon, R.T., & Norman, A. (2006). Computer-based instruction for purchasing skills. *Education and Training in Developmental Disabilities, 41,* 252–263.

Bahr, C., Kinzer, C.K., & Reith, H. (1991). An analysis of the effects of teacher training and student grouping on reading comprehension skills among mildly handicapped high school students using computer-assisted instruction. *Journal of Special Education Technology, 11*(3), 136–154.

Bahr, C.M., & Rieth, H.J. (1991). Effects of cooperative, competitive, and individualistic goals on student achievement using computer-based drill-and-practice. *Journal of Special Education Technology, 11*(1), 33–48.

Bateman, B.D., & Herr, C.M. (2006). *Writing measurable IEP goals and objectives.* Verona, WI: IEP Resources.

Bates, P.E., Cuvo, T., Miner, C.A., & Korabek, C.A. (2001). A simulated and community-based instruction involving persons with mild and moderate mental retardation. *Research in Developmental Disabilities, 22,* 95–115.

Beakley, B.A., & Yoder, S.L. (1998). Middle schoolers learn community skills. *TEACHING Exceptional Children, 30*(3), 16–21.

Becker, R.L. (2000). *Becker Work Adjustment Profile* (2nd ed.). Columbus, OH: Elbern Publications.

Bell, K., & Young, R.K. (1990). Facilitating mainstreaming of students with behavioral disorders using classwide peer tutoring. *School Psychology Review, 19,* 564–573.

Bennett. R.L. (2006). *Bennett's Mechanical Comprehension Test.* San Antonio, TX: Pearson.

Benz, M.R., Lindstrom, L., & Yovanoff, P. (2000). Improving graduation and employment outcomes of students with disabilities: Predictive factors and student perspectives. *Exceptional Children, 66,* 509–529.

Benz, M.R., Yovanoff, P., & Doren, B. (1997). School-to-work components that predict postschool success for students with and without disabilities. *Exceptional Children, 63*, 151–165.

Berg, W.K., Wacker, D.P., Ebbers, B., Wiggins, B., Fowler, M., & Wilkes, P. (1995). A demonstration of generalization of performance across settings, materials, and motor responses for students with profound mental retardation. *Behavior Modification, 19*, 119–143.

Blackorby, J., Hancock, G.R., & Siegel, S. (1993). *Human capital and structural explanations of postschool success for youth with disabilities: A latent variable exploration of the National Longitudinal Transition Study.* Menlo Park, CA: SRI International.

Blackorby, J., & Wagner, M. (1996). Longitudinal postschool outcomes of youth with disabilities: Findings from the National Longitudinal Transition Study. *Exceptional Children, 62*, 399–413.

Bost, L.W., & Riccomini, P.J. (2006). Effective instruction: An inconspicuous strategy for dropout prevention. *Remedial and Special Education, 27*, 301–311.

Boyle, J.R. (2000). The effects of a Venn diagram strategy on the literal, inferential, and relational comprehension of students with mild disabilities. *Learning Disabilities: A Multidisciplinary Journal, 10*, 5–13.

Branham, R.S., Collins, B.C., Schuster, J.W., & Kleinert, H. (1999). Teaching community skills to students with moderate disabilities: Comparing combined techniques of classroom simulation, videotape modeling, and community-based instruction. *Education and Training in Mental Retardation and Developmental Disabilities, 34*, 170–181.

Briggs, A., Alberto, P., Sharpton, W., Berlin, K., McKinley, C., & Ritts, C. (1990). Generalized use of a self-operated audio prompting system. *Education and Training in Mental Retardation, 25*, 381–389.

Brolin, D.A. (2004). *Life-centered career education performance and knowledge battery.* Reston, VA: Council for Exceptional Children.

Brolin, D.E. (1989). *Life-centered career education: A competency-based approach* (3rd ed.). Reston, VA: Council for Exceptional Children.

Brown, L., Nisbet, J., Ford, A., Sweet, M., Shiraga, B., York, J., et al. (1983). The critical need for nonschool instruction in educational programs for severely handicapped students. *Journal of the Association for the Severely Handicapped, 8*, 71–77.

Burcroff, T.L., Radogna, D.M., & Wright, E.H. (2003). Community forays: Addressing students' functional skills in inclusive settings. *TEACHING Exceptional Children, 35*(5), 52–57.

Cameto, R., Levine, P., & Wagner, M. (2004). *Transition planning for students with disabilities: A special topic report of findings from the National Longitudinal Transition Study 2 (NLTS2).* Retrieved April 4, 2011, from http://eric.ed.gov/PDFS/ED496547.pdf

Carl D. Perkins Vocational and Applied Technology Education Act Amendments of 1990, PL 101-392, 104 Statutes at Large 753-804, 806-834.

Carr, S.C., & Punzo, R.P. (1993). The effects of self-monitoring of academic accuracy and productivity on the performance of students with behavioral disorders. *Behavioral Disorders, 18*, 241–250.

Carter, E.W., Ditchman, N., Sun, Y., Trainor, A.A., Sweeden, B., & Owens, L. (2010). Summer employment and community experiences of transition-age youth with severe disabilities. *Exceptional Children, 76*, 194–212.

Cataldi, E.F., Laird, J., & KewalRamani, A. (2009). *High school dropout and completion rates in the United States: 2007* (NCES 2009-064). Retrieved April 4, 2011, from http://nces.ed.gov/pub search/pubsinfo.asp?pubid=2009064

Certo, N.J., Luecking, R.G., Courey, S., Brown, L., Murphy, S., & Mautz, D. (2008). Plugging the policy gap at the point of transition for individuals with severe intellectual disabilities: An argument for a seamless transition and federal entitlement to long-term support. *Research and Practice for Persons with Severe Disabilities, 33*, 85–95.

Certo, N., Mezzullo, K., & Hunter, D. (1985). The effect of total task chain training on the acquisition of busperson job skills at a full service community restaurant. *Education and Training of the Mentally Retarded, 20*, 148–156.

Cihak, D.F., Alberto, P.A., Kessler, K.B., & Taber, T.A. (2004). An investigation of instructional scheduling arrangements for community-based instruction. *Research in Developmental Disabilities, 25*, 67–88.

Cihak, D., & Grim, J. (2008). Teaching students with autism spectrum disorder and moderate intellectual disabilities to use counting-on strategies to enhance independent purchasing skills. *Research in Autism Spectrum Disorders, 1,* 716–727.

Cihak, D.F., Kessler, K.B., & Alberto, P.A. (2007). Generalized use of a handheld prompting system. *Research in Developmental Disabilities, 28,* 397–408.

Clark, G.M. (1996). Transition planning assessment for secondary-level students with learning disabilities. *Journal of Learning Disabilities, 29,* 79–92.

Clark, G., & Patton, J. (2009). *Transition Planning Inventory–Revised.* Austin, TX: PRO-ED.

Clark, G.M., Patton, J.R., & Moulton, L.R. (2000). *Informal assessments for transition planning.* Austin, TX: PRO-ED.

Colorado Department of Education. (2001). *Charting a course for the future: A transition toolkit.* Retrieved April 4, 2011, from http://www.cde.state.co.us/cdesped/TK.asp

Colyer, S., & Collins, B. (1996). Using natural cues within prompt levels to teach the next dollar strategy to students with disabilities. *The Journal of Special Education, 30,* 305–318.

Cook, B.G., Tankersley, M., Cook, L., & Landrum, T.J. (2008). Evidence-based practices in special education: Some practical considerations. *Intervention in School and Clinic, 44*(2), 69–75.

Cooper, J.O., Heron, T.E., & Heward, W.L. (2007). *Applied behavior analysis* (2nd ed.). Upper Saddle River, NJ: Pearson.

Cross, T., Cooke, N.L., Wood, W.M., & Test, D.W. (1999). Comparison of the effects of *MAPS* and *ChoiceMaker* on student self-determination skills. *Education and Training in Mental Retardation and Developmental Disabilities, 34,* 499–510.

Curriculum Associates. (2010). *Brigance Transition Skills Inventory.* North Billerica, MA: Author.

Cuvo, A.J., & Klatt, K.P. (1992). Effects of community-based, videotape, and flash card instruction of community-referenced sight words on students with mental retardation. *Journal of Applied Behavior Analysis, 25,* 499–512.

Denny, P.J., & Test, D.W. (1995). Using the one-more-than technique to teach money counting to individuals with moderate mental retardation: A systematic replication. *Education & Treatment of Children, 18,* 422–432.

Diebold, T., & Waldron, M. (1988). Designing instructional formats: The effects of verbal and pictorial components on hearing-impaired students' comprehension of science concepts. *American Annals of the Deaf, 133,* 30–35.

DiGangi, S.A., & Maag, J.W. (1992). A component analysis of self-management training with behaviorally disordered youth. *Behavioral Disorders, 17,* 281–290.

DiPipi-Hoy, C., Jitendra, A., & Kern, L. (2009). Effects of time management instruction on adolescents' ability to self-manage time in a vocational setting. *Journal of Special Education, 43,* 145–159.

Enderlee, J., & Severson, S. (2003). *Enderlee-Severson Transition Rating Scales* (3rd ed.). Morehead, MN: ESTR Publications.

Ferguson, B., & McDonnell, J. (1991). A comparison of serial and concurrent sequencing strategies in teaching generalized grocery item location to students with moderate handicaps. *Education and Training in Mental Retardation, 26,* 292–304.

Fontana, J.L., Scruggs, T., & Mastropieri, M.A. (2007). Mnemonic strategy instruction in inclusive secondary social studies classes. *Remedial and Special Education, 28,* 345–355.

Forest, M., & Lusthaus, E. (1990). Everyone belongs with MAPS action planning system. *TEACHING Exceptional Children, 22,* 32–35.

Gallaher, K.M., van Kraayenoord, C.E., Jobling, A., & Moni, K.B. (2002). Reading with Abby: A case study of individual tutoring with a young adult with Down syndrome. *Down Syndrome Research and Practice, 8*(2), 59–66.

Gardner, M.F. (1989). *Test of Academic Achievement Skills–Revised (TAAS-R).* Novato, CA: Academic Therapy Publications.

Gaule, K., Nietupski, J., & Certo, N. (1985). Teaching supermarket shopping skills using an adaptive shopping list. *Education and Training of the Mentally Retarded, 20,* 53–59.

German, S.L., Martin, J.E., Marshall, L.H., & Sale, P.R. (2000). Promoting self-determination: Using *Take Action* to teach goal attainment. *Career Development for Exceptional Individuals, 23,* 27–38.

Gersten, R., Fuchs, L.S., Compton, D., Coyne, M., Greenwood, C., & Innocenti, M.S. (2005). Quality indicators for group experimental and quasi-experimental research in special education. *Exceptional Children, 71,* 149–164.

Gilliam, J.E. (1994). *Work Adjustment Inventory: Measures of job-related temperament.* Austin, TX: PRO-ED.

Glutting, J.J., & Wilkinson, G.S. (2003). *Wide Range Interest and Occupation Test* (2nd ed.). Austin, TX: PRO-ED.

Grossen, B., & Carnine, D. (1990). Diagramming a logic strategy: Effects on difficult problem types and transfer. *Learning Disabilities Quarterly, 13,* 168–182.

Halpern, A. (1985). Transition: A look at the foundations. *Exceptional Children, 51,* 479–486.

Halpern, A. (1992). Transition: Old wine in new bottles. *Exceptional Children, 58,* 202–211.

Hamill, L.B. (2002). *Teaching students with moderate to severe disabilities: An applied approach for inclusive environments.* Upper Saddle River, NJ: Merrill Prentice Hall.

Haring, T.G., Breen, C.G., Weiner, J., Kennedy, C.H., & Bednersh, F. (1995). Using videotape modeling to facilitate generalized purchasing skills. *Journal of Behavioral Education, 5,* 29–53.

Harrington, T.F., & O'Shea, A.J. (2000). *The Harrington-O'Shea Career Decision Making System–Revised.* Circle Pines, MN: American Guidance Service.

Hasazi, S., Gordon, L., & Roe, C. (1985). Factors associated with the employment status of handicapped youth exiting high school from 1979–1983. *Exceptional Children, 51,* 455–469.

Hawkins, J. (1988). Antecedent pausing as a direct instruction tactic for adolescents with severe behavioral disorders. *Behavioral Disorders, 13,* 263–272.

Hawkins, J., & Brady, M.P. (1994). The effects of independent and peer guided practice during instructional pauses on the academic performance of students with mild handicaps. *Education & Treatment of Children, 17,* 1–28.

Higgins, K., Boone, R., & Lovitt, T.C. (1996). Hypertext support for remedial students and students with learning disabilities. *Journal of Learning Disabilities, 29,* 402–412.

Hock, M.F., Pulvers, K.A., Deshler, D.D., & Schumaker, J.B. (2001). The effects of an after-school tutoring program on the academic performance of at-risk students and students with LD. *Remedial and Special Education, 22,* 172–186.

Hoffman, A., & Field, S. (2005). *Steps to self-determination.* Austin, TX: PRO-ED.

Holland, J. (1994). *Self-Directed Search Form R* (4th ed.). Odessa, FL: Psychological Assessment Resources.

Holland, J. (1996). *Self-Directed Search Form E* (4th ed.). Odessa, FL: Psychological Assessment Resources.

Holland, J., & Powell, A. (1994). *Self-Directed Search: Career Explorer.* Odessa, FL: Psychological Assessment Resources.

Hollingsworth, M., & Woodward, J. (1993). Integrating learning: Explicit strategies and their role in problem-solving instructions for students with learning disabilities. *Exceptional Children, 59,* 444–455.

Horner, R.H., Carr, E.G., Halle, J., McGee, G., Odom, S., & Wolery, M. (2005). The use of single-subject research to identify evidence-based practice in special education. *Exceptional Children, 71,* 165–179.

Horton, S., & Lovitt, T.C. (1988). Teaching geography to high school students with academic deficits: Effects of a computerized map tutorial. *Learning Disability Quarterly, 11,* 371–379.

Horton, S., Lovitt, T.C., & Bergerud, D. (1990). The effectiveness of graphic organizers for three classifications of secondary students in content area classes. *Journal of Learning Disabilities, 23,* 12–29.

Hughes, C., Carter, E.W., Hughes, T., Bradford, E., & Copeland, S.R. (2002). Effects of instructional versus non-instructional roles on the social interactions of high school students. *Education & Training in Mental Retardation, 37,* 146–162.

Hyerle, D. (1996). *Visual tools for constructing knowledge.* Alexandria, VA: Association for Supervision and Curriculum Development.

Hyerle, D. (2000). *A field guide to using visual tools.* Alexandria, VA: Association for Supervision and Curriculum Development.

Individuals with Disabilities Education Act (IDEA) of 1990, PL 101-476, 20 U.S.C. §§ 1400 *et seq.*

Individuals with Disabilities Education Act Amendments (IDEA) of 1997, PL 105-17, 20 U.S.C. §§ 1400 *et seq.*

Individuals with Disabilities Education Improvement Act of 2004, PL 108-446, 20 U.S.C. §§ 1400 *et seq.*

Izzo, M.V., Yurick, A., Nagaraja, H.N., & Novak, J.A. (2010). Effects of a 21st-century curriculum on students' information technology and transition skills. *Career Development for Exceptional Individuals, 33,* 95–105.

Job Training Reform Amendments of 1992, PL 102-367, 20 U.S.C. §§ 1501 *et seq.*

Keyes, M.W., & Owens-Johnson, L. (2003). Developing person-centered IEPs. *Intervention in School and Clinic, 38,* 145–152.

Kluth, P. (2000). Community-referenced learning and the inclusive classroom. *Remedial and Special Education, 21,* 19–26.

Kochhar-Bryant, C.A., & Bassett, D.S. (2002). Challenge and promise in aligning transition and standards-based education. In C.A. Kochhar-Bryant & D.S. Bassett (Eds.), *Aligning transition and standards-based education: Issues and strategies* (pp. 1–24). Arlington, VA: Council for Exceptional Children.

Kohler, P.D. (1993). Best practices in transition: Substantiated or implied? *Career Development for Exceptional Individuals, 16,* 107–121.

Kohler, P.D. (1996). *A taxonomy for transition programming: Linking research and practice.* Champaign, IL: Transition Research Institute, University of Illinois.

Kohler, P.D., DeStefano, L., Wermuth, T.R., Grayson, T.E., & McGinty, S. (1994). An analysis of exemplary transition programs: How and why are they selected? *Career Development for Exceptional Individuals, 17,* 187–202.

Kohler, P.D., & Field, S. (2003). Transition-focused education: Foundation for the future. *Journal of Special Education, 37,* 174–183.

Konrad, M., & Test, D.W. (2004). Teaching middle-school students with disabilities to use an IEP template. *Career Development for Exceptional Individuals, 27,* 101–124.

Konrad, M., & Test, D.W. (2007). Effects of GO FOR IT...NOW! strategy instruction on the written IEP goal articulation and paragraph-writing skills of middle school students with disabilities. *Remedial and Special Education, 28,* 277–291.

Konrad, M., & Test, D.W. (2007). GO FOR IT...NOW! Unpublished form.

Kulik, J.A. (2003, May). *Effects of using instructional technology in elementary and secondary schools: What controlled evaluation studies say.* Arlington, VA: SRI International.

Kulik, J.A., & Kulik, C.L.C. (1987). Review of recent research literature on computer-based instruction. *Contemporary Educational Psychology, 12,* 222–230.

Laird, J., Cataldi, E.F., KewalRamani, A., & Chapman, C. (2008). *Dropout and completion rates in the United States: 2006.* Retrieved April 4, 2011, from http://nces.ed.gov/pubsearch/pubsinfo .asp?pubid=2008053

Lancioni, G.E., & O'Reilly, M. (2001). Self-management of instruction cues for occupation: Review of studies with people with severe and profound developmental disabilities. *Research in Developmental Disabilities, 22,* 41–65.

Lapan, R.T. (2004). *Career development across the K–16 Years: Bridging the present to satisfying and successful futures.* Alexandria, VA: American Counseling Association.

Levinson, E.M. (1994). Current vocational assessment models for students with disabilities. *Journal of Counseling and Development, 73,* 94–101.

Lindstrom, L., Doren, B., Metheny, J., Johnson, P., & Zane, C. (2007). Transition to employment: Role of the family in career development. *Exceptional Children, 73,* 348–366.

Liptak, R. (2006). *Job Search Attitude Survey* (3rd ed.). St. Paul, MN: JIST Publishing.

Luzzo, D.A., Rottinghaus, P.J., & Zytowski, D.G. (2006). *Kuder Career Planning System.* Adel, IA: Kuder, Inc.

MacArthur, C.A., & Haynes, J.B. (1995). Student assistant for learning from text (SALT): A hypermedia reading aid. *Journal of Learning Disabilities, 28,* 150–159.

Malouf, D.B., Wizer, D.R., Pilato, V.H., & Grogan, M.M. (1990). Computer-assisted instruction with small groups of mildly handicapped students. *Journal of Special Education, 24,* 51–68.

Marshall, L.H., Martin, J.E., Maxson, L.M., Miller, T.L., McGill, T., Hughes, W.M., et al. (1999). *Take action: Making goals happen.* Longmont, CO: Sopris West.

Martella, R., Marchand-Martella, N.E., Young, K.R., & MacFarlane, C.A. (1995). Determining the collateral effects of peer tutor training on a student with severe disabilities. *Behavior Modification, 19,* 170–191.

Martin, J.E., Huber Marshall, L., & Sale, P. (2004). A 3-year study of middle, junior high, and high school IEP meetings. *Exceptional Children, 70,* 285–297.

Martin, J.E., Marshall, L.H., & Maxson, L.L. (1993). Transition policy: Infusing self-determination and self-advocacy into transition programs. *Career Development for Exceptional Individuals, 16,* 53–61.

Martin, J.E., Marshall, L.H., Maxson, L.M., & Jerman, P.L. (1996). *The self-directed IEP.* Longmont, CO: Sopris West.

Martin, J.E., Mithaug, D.E., Cox, P., Peterson, L.Y., Van Dycke, J.L., & Cash, M.E. (2003). Increasing self-determination: Teaching students to plan, work, evaluate, and adjust. *Exceptional Children, 69,* 431–447.

Martin, J.E., Van Dycke, J.L., Christensen, W.R., Greene, B.A., Gardner, J.E., & Lovett, D.L. (2006). Increasing student participation in their transition IEP meetings: Establishing the *Self-Directed IEP* as an evidenced-based practice. *Exceptional Children, 72,* 299–316.

Martin, J. E., Van Dycke, J., D'Ottavio, M., & Nickerson, K. (2007). The student-directed summary of performance: Increasing student and family involvement in the transition planning process. *Career Development for Exceptional Children, 30,* 13–26.

Mastropieri, M.A., & Scruggs, T.E. (1998). Enhancing school success with mnemonic strategies. *Intervention in School & Clinic, 33,* 201–208.

Mazzotti, V. (2007, January). *Tranistion-rich IEPs.* Ft. Worth, TX.

Mazzotti, V.L., Rowe, D.A., Kelley, K.R., Test, D.W., Fowler, C.H., Kohler, P.D., & Kortering, L.J. (2009). Linking transition assessment and post-secondary goals: Key elements in the secondary transition planning process. *TEACHING Exceptional Children, 42,* 44–51.

McCarney, S.B., & Anderson, P.D. (2000). *Transition Behavior Scale* (2nd ed.). Columbia, MO: Hawthorne.

McDonnell, J., & Ferguson, B. (1989). A comparison of time delay and decreasing prompt hierarchy strategies in teaching banking skills to students with moderate handicaps. *Journal of Applied Behavior Analysis, 22,* 85–91.

McDonnell, J., Mathot-Buckner, C., Thorson, N., & Fister, S. (2001). Supporting the inclusion of students with moderate and severe disabilities in junior high school general education classes: The effects of classwide peer tutoring, multi-element curriculum, and accommodations. *Education & Treatment of Children, 24,* 141–160.

Mechling, L.C. (2004). Effects of multimedia, computer-based instruction on grocery shopping fluency. *Journal of Special Education Technology, 19*(1), 23–34.

Mechling, L.C., & Cronin, B. (2006). Computer-based video instruction to teach the use of augmentative and alternative communication devices for ordering at fast food restaurants. *The Journal of Special Education, 39,* 234–245.

Mechling, L.C., Gast, D.L., & Langone, J. (2002). Computer-based video instruction to teach persons with moderate intellectual disabilities to read grocery aisle signs and locate items. *The Journal of Special Education, 35,* 224–240.

Mechling, L.C., & Ortega-Hurndon, F. (2007). Computer-based video instruction to teach young adults with moderate intellectual disabilities to perform multiple step, job tasks in a generalized setting. *Education and Training in Mental Retardation and Developmental Disabilities, 42,* 24–37.

Miller, K.J. (1995). Cooperative conversations: The effect of cooperative learning on conversational interaction. *American Annals of the Deaf, 140,* 28–37.

Mithaug, D.E., Horiuchi, C.N., & Fanning, P.N. (1985). A report on the Colorado statewide follow-up survey of special education students. *Exceptional Children, 51,* 397–404.

Montague, M. (1988). Job-related social skills training for adolescents with handicaps. *Career Development for Exceptional Individuals, 11,* 27–41.

Mooney, P., Ryan, J.B., Uhing, B.M., Reid, R., & Epstein, M.H. (2005). A review of self management interventions targeting academic outcomes for students with emotional and behavioral disorders. *Journal of Behavioral Education, 14,* 203–221.

Morgan, R.L., Morgan, R.B., Despain, D., & Vasquez, E. (2006). I can search for jobs on the internet: A website that helps youth in transition identify preferred employment. *TEACHING Exceptional Children, 38*(6), 6–11.

Morningstar, M.E., Frey, B.B., Noonan, P.M., Ng, J., Clavenna-Deane, B., Graves, P., et al. (2010). A preliminary investigation of the relationship of transition preparation and self-determination for students with disabilities in postsecondary educational settings. *Career Development for Exceptional Individuals, 33,* 80–94.

Morse, T.E., & Schuster, J.W. (2000). Teaching elementary students with moderate intellectual disabilities how to shop for groceries. *Exceptional Children, 66,* 273–288.

Myers, J.B., & Briggs, K.C. (1988). *Myers-Briggs Type Indicator: Form M.* Palo Alto, CA: Consulting Psychological Press.

National Center for Special Education Research. (2005). *National Longitudinal Transition Study 2.* Retrieved February 19, 2011, from http://www.nlts2.org/

National Secondary Transition Technical Assistance Center. (2009). *Indicator 13 checklist.* Retrieved April 4, 2011, from http://www.nsttac.org/indicator13/indicator13_checklist.aspx

National Secondary Transition Technical Assistance Center. (2008). *Lesson plan library.* Retrieved from http://www.nsttac.org/LessonPlanLibrary/StudentFocusedPlanning.aspx

Neath, J., & Bolton, B. (2008). *Work Personality Profile.* Austin, TX: PRO-ED.

Nelson, J.R., Smith, D.J., & Dodd, J.M. (1994). The effects of learning strategy instruction on the completion of job applications by students with learning disabilities. *Journal of Learning Disabilities, 27,* 104–110.

Neubert, D.A. (2003). The role of assessment in the transition to adult life process for students with disabilities. *Exceptionality, 11,* 63–75.

Newman, L., Wagner, M., Cameto, R., & Knokey, A.M. (2009). *The post-high school outcomes of youth with disabilities up to 4 years after high school. A report of findings from the National Longitudinal Transition Study 2.* Retrieved April 4, 2011, from www.nlts2.org/reports/2009_04/nlts2_report_2009_04_complete.pdf

Nietupski, J., Hamre-Nietupski, S., Curtin, S., & Shrikanth, K. (1997). A review of curricular research in severe disabilities from 1976–1995 in six selected journals. *The Journal of Special Education, 31,* 36–55.

No Child Left Behind Act of 2001, PL 107-110, 115 Stat. 1425, 20 U.S.C. §§ 6301 *et seq.*

Odom, S.L., Brantlinger, E., Gersten, R., Horner, R.H., Thompson, B., & Harris, K.R. (2005). Research in special education: Scientific methods and evidence-based practices. *Exceptional Children, 71,* 137–148.

Okolo, C.M. (1992). The effects of computer-based attribution retraining on the attributions, persistence, and mathematics computation of students with learning disabilities. *Journal of Learning Disabilities, 25,* 327–334.

Okolo, C.M., Bahr, C.M., & Rieth, H.J. (1993). A retrospective view of computer-based instruction. *Journal of Special Education Technology, 12*(1), 1–27.

O'Melia, M., & Rosenberg, M. (1994). Effects of cooperative homework teams on the acquisition of mathematics skills by secondary students with mild disabilities. *Exceptional Children, 60,* 538–548.

PACER Center, ALLIANCE National Parent Technical Assistance Center. (2007). *Parent tips for transition planning.* Retrieved April 1, 2011, from http://www.pacer.org/publications/pdfs/ALL14.pdf

Parker, R.M. (2002). *Occupational Aptitude Survey* (3rd ed.). Austin, TX: PRO-ED.

Pattavina, S., Bergstrom, T., Marchand-Martella, N.E., & Martella, R.C. (1992). "Moving on": Learning to cross streets independently. *TEACHING Exceptional Children, 25*(1), 32–35.

Porfeli, E.J., Hartung, P.J., & Vondracek, F.W. (2008). Children's vocational development: A research rationale. *Career Development Quarterly, 57,* 25–37.

Posgrow, S. (1990). A Socratic approach to using computers with at-risk students. *Educational Leadership, 47*(5), 61.

Postsecondary Education Programs Network. (2008). *iTransition.* Retrieved April 4, 2011, from http://itransition.pepnet.org/

Powers, L.E., Turner, A., Matuszewski, J., Wilson, R., & Phillips, A. (2001). TAKE CHARGE for the future: A controlled field-test of a model to promote student involvement in transition planning. *Career Development for Exceptional Individuals, 24,* 89–103.

PsychCorp. (2010). AIMSweb Pro Reading. San Antonio, TX: NCS Pearson.

Rafferty, L.A. (2010). Step-by-step: Teaching students to self-monitor. *TEACHING Exceptional Children, 43*(2), 50–58.

Rehabilitation Act Amendments of 1992, PL 102-569, 29 U.S.C. §§ 701 *et seq.*

Reid, R., Trout, A.L., & Schartz, M. (2005). Self-regulation interventions for children with attention deficit/hyperactivity disorder. *Exceptional Children, 71,* 361–377.

Repetto, J.B., Pankaskie, S., Hankins, A., & Schwartz, S.E. (1997). Promising practices in dropout prevention and transition for students with mild disabilities. *Journal of At Risk Issues, 4,* 19–29.

Rieth, H., Bahr, C., Okolo, C.M., Polsgrove, L., & Eckert, R. (1988). An analysis of the impact of microcomputers on the secondary special education classroom ecology. *Journal of Educational Computing Research, 4,* 425–441.

Riffel, L.A., Wehmeyer, M.L., Turnbull, A.P., Lattimore, J., Davies, D., Stock, S., et al. (2005). Promoting independent performance of transition-related tasks using a palmtop PC-based self-directed visual and auditory prompting system. *Journal of Special Education Technology, 20*(2), 5–14.

Roessler, R. (2000). Three recommendations to improve transition planning in the IEP. *The Journal for Vocational Special Needs Education, 22*(2), 31–36.

Roessler, R.T., Brolin, D.E., & Johnson, J.M. (1990). Factors affecting employment success and quality. *Career Development for Exceptional Individuals, 13,* 95–107.

Rosenburg, H., & Brady, M. (2000). *JOBS: Job observation and behavior scale.* Wooddale, IL: Stoelting.

Rusch, F.R., & Braddock, D. (2004). Adult day programs versus supported employment (1988–2002): Spending and service practices of mental retardation and developmental disabilities state agencies. *Research and Practice for Persons with Severe Disabilities, 29,* 237–242.

Rusch, F.R., Kohler, P.D., & Hughes, L. (1992). An analysis of OSERS-sponsored secondary special education and transitional services research. *Career Development for Exceptional Individuals, 15,* 121–143.

Schloss, P.J., Kobza, S.A., & Alper, S. (1997). The use of peer tutoring for the acquisition of functional math skills among students with moderate retardation. *Education & Treatment of Children, 20,* 189–208.

School-to-Work Opportunities Act of 1994, PL 103-239, 20 U.S.C. §§ 6101 *et seq.*

Scruggs, T.E., Mastropieri, M.A., & Richter, L. (1985). Peer tutoring with behaviorally disordered students: Social and academic benefits. *Behavioral Disorders, 10,* 283–294.

Shafer, M.S., Inge, K.J., & Hill, J. (1986). Acquisition, generalization, and maintenance of automated banking skills. *Education and Training of the Mentally Retarded, 21,* 265–272.

Shevin, M., & Klein, N.K. (1984). The importance of choice-making skills for students with severe disabilities. *Journal of the Association for Persons with Severe Handicaps, 9,* 159–166.

Shevin, M., & Klein, N.K. (2004). Classic TASH article III: The importance of choice-making skills for students with severe disabilities. *Research and Practice for Persons with Severe Disabilities, 29,* 161–168.

Sitlington, P. (2008). Students with reading and writing challenges: Using informal assessment to assist in planning for the transition adult life. *Reading & Writing Quarterly, 24,* 77–100.

Sitlington, P.L., & Clark, G. (2001). Career/vocational assessment: A critical component of transition planning. *Assessment for Effective Intervention, 26,* 5–22.

Sitlington, P., & Clark, G. (2007). The transition assessment process and IDEIA 2004. *Assessment for Effective Intervention, 32,* 133–142.

Sitlington, P.L., Neubert, D.A., & Leconte, P.J. (1997). Transition assessment: The position of the Division for Career Development and Transition. *Career Development for Exceptional Individuals, 20,* 69–79.

Sitlington, P., & Payne, E. (2004). Information needed by postsecondary education: Can we provide it as part of the transition assessment process? *Learning Disabilities: A Contemporary Journal, 2*(2), 1–14.

Smith, R.L., Collins, B.C., Schuster, J.W., & Kleinert, H. (1999). Teaching table cleaning skills to secondary students with moderate/server disabilities: Facilitating observational learning during instructional downtime. *Education and Training in Mental Retardation and Developmental Disabilities, 34,* 342–353.

Souza, G., & Kennedy, C.H. (2003). Facilitating social interactions in the community for a transition-age student with severe disabilities. *Journal of Positive Behavior Interventions, 5,* 179–182.

Sparrow, S.S., Cicchetti, D.V., & Balla, D.A. (2005). *Vineland Adaptive Behavior Scales* (2nd ed.). Circle Pines, MN: American Guidance Services.

Staub, D., Spaulding, M., Peck, C.A., Gallucci, C., & Schwartz, I.S. (1996). Using nondisabled peers to support the inclusion of students with disabilities at the junior high school level. *Journal of the Association for Persons with Severe Handicaps, 21,* 194–205.

Stokes, T.F., & Baer, D.M. (1977). An implicit technology of generalization. *Journal of Applied Behavior Analysis, 10,* 349–367.

Synatschk, K.O., Clark, G.M., & Patton, J.R. (2008). *Informal assessments for transition: Independent living and community participation.* Austin, TX: PRO-ED.

Taber, T.A., Alberto, P.A., Hughes, M., & Seltzer, A. (2002). A strategy for students with moderate disabilities when lost in the community. *Research and Practice for Persons with Severe Disabilities, 27,* 141–152.

Tateyama-Sniezek, K.M. (1990). Cooperative learning: Does it improve the academic achievement of students with handicaps? *Exceptional Children, 56,* 426–437.

Taylor, P., Collins, B.C., Schuster, J.W., & Kleinert, H. (2002) Teaching laundry skills to high school students with disabilities: Generalization of targeted skills and nontargeted information. *Education and Training in Mental Retardation and Developmental Disabilities, 37,* 172–183.

Test, D.W., Fowler, C.H., Richter, S.M., White, J., Mazzotti, V., Walker, A.R., et al. (2009a). Evidence-based practices in secondary transition. *Career Development for Exceptional Individuals, 32,* 115–128.

Test, D.W., Fowler, C.H., White, J., Richter, S., & Walker, A. (2009b). Evidence-based secondary transition practices for enhancing school completion. *Exceptionality, 17,* 16–29.

Test, D.W., Mazzotti, V.L., Mustian, A.L., Fowler, C.H., Kortering, L.J., & Kohler, P.H. (2009c). Evidence-based secondary transition predictors for improving post-school outcomes for students with disabilities. *Career Development for Exceptional Individuals, 32,* 160–181.

Thompson, J.R., Bryant, B.R., Campbell, E.M., Craig, E.M., Hughes, C., Rotholz, D.R., et al. (2004). *Supports Intensity Scale.* Washington, DC: American Association on Intellectual and Developmental Disabilities.

Trask-Tyler, S.A., Grossi, T.A., & Heward, W.A. (1994). Teaching young adults with developmental disabilities and visual impairments to use tape-recorded recipes: Acquisition, generalization, and maintenance of cooking skills. *Journal of Behavioral Education, 4,* 283–311.

U.S. Department of Defense. (2005). *Armed Services Vocational Aptitude Battery* (ASVAB). Seaside, CA: Defense Manpower Data Center Monterey Bay.

U.S. Department of Education. (2003). *Twenty-fifth annual report to Congress on the implementation of the Individuals with Disabilities Education Act.* Washington, DC: Author.

U. S. Department of Education Office of Special Education Programs. (2009). *Part B State Performance Plan (SPP) and Annual Performance Report (APR): Part B indicator measurement table.* Washington, DC: U.S. Department of Education.

U.S. Department of Labor. (2001). *O*NET Interest Profiler.* Washington, DC: Author.

Vandercook, T. (1991). Leisure instruction outcomes: Criterion performance, positive interactions, and acceptance by typical high school peers. *The Journal of Special Education, 25,* 320–339.

Van Laarhoven, T., Johnson, J.W., Van Laarhoven-Myers, T., Grider, K.L., & Grider, K.M. (2009). The effectiveness of using a video iPod as a prompting device in employment settings. *Journal of Behavioral Education, 18,* 119–141.

Van Reusen, A.K., & Bos, C.S. (1994). Facilitating student participation in individualized education programs through motivation strategy instruction. *Exceptional Children, 60,* 466–475.

Van Reusen, A.K., Bos, C., & Schumaker, J.B. (1994). *Self-advocacy strategy for education and transition planning.* Lawrence, KS: Edge Enterprises.

Wagner, M., Newman, L., Cameto, R., Garza, N., & Levine, P. (2005). *After high school: A first look at the postschool experiences of youth with disabilities: A report from the National Longitudinal Transition Study 2 (NLTS2).* Retrieved April 4, 2011, from http://www.eric.ed.gov/PDFS/ED494935.pdf

Walker, A.R., Fowler, C.H., Kortering, L.J., & Rowe, D. (2010). *Transition Assessment Toolkit* (2nd ed.). Charlotte, NC: National Secondary Transition Technical Assistance Center.

Ward, M.J., & Kohler, P.D. (1996). Promoting self-determination for individuals with disabilities: Content and process. In L.E. Powers, G.H.S. Singer, & J. Sowers (Eds.), *On the road to autonomy: Promoting self-competence in children and youth with disabilities* (pp. 275–290). Baltimore: Paul H. Brookes Publishing Co.

Wechsler, D. (2004). *Wechsler Intelligence Scale for Children–IV.* San Antonio, TX: Psychological Corporation.

Wehman, P. (2011). *Essentials of transition planning.* Baltimore: Paul H. Brookes Publishing Co.

Wehmeyer, M., Lawrence, M., Garner, N., Soukup, J., & Palmer, S. (2004). *Whose future is it anyway? A student-directed transition planning process.* Retrieved from http://education.ou.edu/zarrow/files/WFCGuide%20Final.pdf

Wehmeyer, M.L., Palmer, S.B., Agran, M., Mithaug, D.E., & Martin, J.E. (2000). Promoting causal agency: The self-determined learning model of instruction. *Exceptional Children, 66,* 439–453.

Wehmeyer, M., & Schwartz, M. (1997). Self-determination and positive adult outcomes: A follow-up study of youth with mental retardation or learning disabilities. *Exceptional Children, 63,* 245–255.

Wehmeyer, M., & Schwartz, M. (1998). The relationship between self-determination and quality of life for adults with mental retardation. *Education and Training in Mental Retardation and Developmental Disabilities, 33,* 3–12.

Wiesen, J.P. (1997). *Wiesen Test of Mechanical Comprehension.* Odessa, FL: Psychological Assessment Resources.

Will, M. (1984). Bridges from school to working life. *Programs for the handicapped.* Washington, DC: Clearinghouse on the Handicapped.

Wissick, C.A., Gardner, J.E., & Langone, J. (1999). Video-based simulations: Considerations for teaching students with developmental disabilities. *Career Development for Exceptional Individuals, 22,* 233–249.

Wolford, P.L., Heward, W.L., & Alber, S.R. (2001). Teaching middle school students with learning disabilities to recruit peer assistance during cooperative learning group activities. *Learning Disabilities Research & Practice, 16,* 161–173.

Wolgemuth, J.R., Cobb, R.B., & Alwell, M. (2008). The effects of mnemonic interventions on academic outcomes for youth with disabilities: A systematic review. *Learning Disabilities Research, 23*(1), 1–10.

Wolgemuth, J.R., Cobb, R.B., & Dugan. J.J. (2007). *The effects of self-management interventions on academic outcomes for youth with disabilities.* Fort Collins, CO: Colorado State University, School of Education.

Wolgemuth, J.R., Trujillo, E., Cobb, R.B., & Alwell, M. (2008). *The effects of visual display interventions on academic outcomes for youth with disabilities: A systematic review.* Fort Collins, CO: Colorado State University.

Wong, B.Y.L., Butler, D.L., Ficzere, S.A., & Kuperis, S. (1997). Teaching adolescents with learning disabilities and low achievers to plan, write, and revise compare-and-contrast essays. *Learning Disabilities Research & Practice, 12,* 2–15.

Woodcock, R.W., McGrew, K.S., & Mather, N. (2000). *Woodcock-Johnson III Tests of Achievement.* Itasca, IL: Riverside.

Woods, L., Sylvester, L., & Martin, J.E. (2010). Student-directed transition planning: Increasing student knowledge and self-efficacy in the transition planning process. *Career Development for Exceptional Individuals, 33,* 106–114.

Wu, P.F., Martin, J.E., & Isbell, S. (2007). *Increasing the engagement of students with visual impairment in their IEP meetings.* Retrieved April 4, 2011, from http://www.ou.edu/content/education/centers-and-partnerships/zarrow/self-determination-education-materials/iep-team-education-module.html

Index

Tables and figures are indicated by *t* or *f*, respectively.